THE GOSPEL OF JESUS CHRISTUS ACCORDING TO PATIENCE WORTH

As found in the book, *The Sorry Tale: A Story of the Time of Christ*, written by Patience Worth and published in June 1917 by Henry Holt and Company.

Edited & Produced by
Keith Ringkamp
2007

Published by lulu.com

Preface by Casper S. Yost
and text from *The Sorry Tale* by Patience Worth
Copyright 1917
by Henry Holt And Company
and first published in June, 1917

Excerpts from *The Case of Patience Worth*
by Walter Franklin Prince
Copyright 1927
by the Boston Society for Psychic Research

The Gospel of Jesus Christus According to Patience Worth
Copyright 2007 by Keith Ringkamp (k_ringkamp@yahoo.com)

All rights reserved. No part of this publication may be reproduced or transmitted in any form or by any means, electronic or mechanical, including photocopy, or any information storage and retrieval system, without permission from the publisher.

Published by lulu.com

ISBN: 978-1-4303-1575-9

Cover Art by Keith Ringkamp

About This Book

In June 1917, Henry Holt and Company published a book over 600 pages long entitled: *The Sorry Tale: A Story of the Time of Christ.* It earned high critical acclaim and was hailed by many as a literary masterpiece. What makes it more amazing is this book was dictated a letter at a time by Patience Worth, a disembodied spirit, through the mediumship of Pearl Curran. *The Sorry Tale* contains an elegant and exquisite depiction of the gospel of Jesus Christ that has been extracted and presented here in this book, *The Gospel of Jesus Christus According to Patience Worth.* This gospel provides novel insights into the life, lessons, and passions of Jesus. It reads like an eyewitness account and includes many fascinating intimate details. Its value lies as a supplement to the four canonical Gospels. This unique gospel is for open-minded individuals who can recognize the word of God, regardless of the channel through which it flows. In each generation, God provides us with an opportunity to cast off the past and hear His word anew. *The Gospel of Jesus Christus According to Patience Worth* is just such an opportunity.

TABLE OF CONTENTS

Forward by Keith J. Ringkamp	vii
The Sorry Tale: Book Reviews	xi
Original Preface to *The Sorry Tale* by Casper S. Yost	xv
Opinion of Clement Wood	xxiv
Editor's Note	xxv
The Gospel of Jesus Christus According to Patience Worth	1

Forward
By Keith J. Ringkamp
March 2007

On the evening of July 8th, 1913, in a home in St. Louis, Missouri, three women were experimenting with an ouija board. As Pearl Curran and a friend moved the stylus aimlessly, the following words spelled themselves out: *Many moons ago I lived - again I come - Patience Worth my name.* The ghostly message surprised the women, but Patience was not through - the stylus continued seeking letters: *Wait, I would speak with thee. If thou shalt live, then so shall I. I make my bread at thy hearth. Good friends, let us be merrie. The time for work is past. Let the Tabby drowse and blink her wisdom to the firelog.* Thus began a rather constant flow of communications by Patience Worth through the fingertips of Pearl Curran.

Over the next few years, many of Worth's communications were published in magazines, newspapers, and in the book *Patience Worth: A Psychic Mystery* by Casper S. Yost.[1] She quickly achieved international fame. She dazzled the world community with her banter, poems, aphorisms, witticisms, essays, and books (she spelled out several of them). She was hailed as a genius, a poet equal to Whitman. She performed a number of extemporaneous literary feats of a highly complex and dexterous nature, the likes of which have not been matched by any other. Her deeds were performed under the watchful and skeptical eyes of various professionals (e.g. journalists, doctors, lawyers, philosophers, psychologists, university professors, etc.) most of whom came away astonished and mystified.[2]

---

[1] Published by Henry Holt and Company, New York, 1916
[2] See *The Case of Patience Worth* by W. F. Prince, University Books, 1964

The popularity of Patience Worth faded like a shooting star. Within a generation, her books went out of print – they never saw a second printing. Her poems and other writings were relegated to obscurity. Pearl Curran died of pneumonia in 1937 without much money or fanfare. Today, only a handful of individuals know about Patience Worth, and only a fraction of those take the time to become seriously acquainted with her writings. Her communications, which total nearly four million words, sit encoded, bound, and largely undisturbed in the archives at the Missouri Historical Society.

Patience Worth claimed to be the spirit of a seventeenth century Englishwoman who traveled to America only to be killed in an Indian raid. Two of her books, *Telka*[3] and *Hope Trueblood*,[4] reinforce that claim as the author of both is familiar with the language and customs of seventeenth century rural England.[5] Patience also referred to herself in more mysterious terms. Once, when questioned about her origin, she gave the following response, *I be like the wind who leaveth not track, but ever 'bout, and yet like to the rain who groweth grain for thee to reap.*

Patience Worth stated that all her *puttings* (one way she described her communications) were religious in nature. She once said, *Do eat that which I offer thee. 'Tis o' Him. I but bear the pack apacked for the carry o' me by Him.* Patience seemed to espouse a mostly Christian creed. In a statement of her beliefs (i.e. Credo), Patience said, *I believe in the all-merciful God, and in His Son as a Sign of His Mercy. I believe in the resurrection of life, for its manifold symbols are before me.* Patience identified her earthly

---

[3] Patience Worth Publishing Co., Inc., N.Y., 1928
[4] Henry Holt and Company, 1918
[5] By contrast, Pearl Curran, an intelligent woman with an eighth grade education, never lived outside parts of Southern and Midwestern America

mission this way: *'Tis the task o' thy handmaid that she set up balms for earth ...*

Patience Worth provides just such a balm in the book *The Sorry Tale: A Story of the Time of Christ*. The story tells about the life of Hatte. He was born to a cast-off slave girl on the outskirts of Bethlehem at roughly the same time as the birth of Jesus. He experienced many hardships and grew to become a hate-filled, bitter man. After leading a life of crime including murder, he lost his sanity upon learning that his father was the Emperor of Rome. Hatte, sometimes referred to as Hate, hounded Jesus throughout the story, attempting to demonstrate the power of hate and folly over love. In the end, as he was being crucified with Jesus, Hatte gave up his hatred and sought God's mercy. Hence, the central theme of the story centers on the transformation of hate into love.

When I first began reading *The Sorry Tale*, I felt a little like Josiah who, upon hearing the words of the recently discovered Book of Law, tore his robes. I didn't tear my clothes, but I did feel the same sense of awe and humility. The tale contains much in the way of worldly and spiritual wisdom, as well as prophecy and revelation. Scattered throughout is Worth's perception of the gospel - it's a gospel overflowing with beauty, wisdom, and truth. It resembles no other account of the life and lessons of Jesus. Fortunately, this gospel is written with sufficient drama and integrity to stand on its own. It has been extracted from the text of *The Sorry Tale* and presented in this book as *The Gospel of Jesus Christus According to Patience Worth* so the reading public may have an opportunity to study it without having to sift through the entire story.

The Worth gospel provides an opportunity to rediscover the essential message of Jesus Christ. This opportunity is expressed in the gospel as a prophecy:

> *And it was true that Jesus had spoken that a man's evil might not be driven forth, but should the man sup of the living waters, behold, the evils might drown. "This is before thee and thou mayest speak it, but the days shall come when this shall rust and man know but the rust's crust. But the might of God shall touch the crumble of rust, and behold, the truth shall be upon thee!"*

The Word of God through the years acquires a veneer of worldly interpretations (i.e. *rust*) that coalesce into creeds, formulas, and dogmas (i.e. *rust's crust*). Worth intends through her gospel not to update or supplant the Word but to aide in recapturing its lifeblood or living essence.

KJR

The Sorry Tale: Book Reviews[1]

The following reviews appeared soon after the publication of *The Sorry Tale*.

Washington *Star,*
"...it is a work of great beauty, a finely noble composition."

The Bookman,
"...a well constructed plot, a sense of the dramatic, a beauty of thought and style, and an excellent picture of the Roman world when the Empire was at its height."

Columbus *Dispatch*,
"Those interested in the gospels should read this book for the way it more firmly impresses the teachings of Jesus and describes the kind of people he lived among."

Los Angeles *Times*
"... perfectly astounding as to style and even more remarkable as to construction."

Philadelphia Book News Monthly
"... There are moments in The Sorry Tale – many of them, even considering its 640 pages – of sensitive recording, memorable description and vivid emotional registry."

---

[1] Source: *The Case of Patience Worth* by W. F. Prince, University Books, 1964

New York *Times*,
"... She invents new miracles, she retells the old ones, she fills out with incidents the lives of Christ and his disciples, but the touching beauty and simple dignity of the figure of Christ are treated always with reverence and there is nothing in the tale to which the most orthodox could object. ... And through it all goes a sense of life, of reality, of having been seen and lived until all its scenes become familiar. ... It is a wonderful, a beautiful, and a noble book ..."

St. Louis *Globe-Democrat*
"The threads of the great plot are woven with consummate skill, never revealing more of that which follows than the author desires, and yet drawing steadily and surely to the tremendous tragedy on Calvary, which is its climax."

Philadelphia *Ledger*
"As dramatic as "Ben-Hur." There is poetic imagination."

Hartford (Ct.) *Courant*
"... As a work of literary composition it is unique and remarkable. ... There is nothing that borders on irreverence in the book. Old miracles are rehearsed and new ones supplied. The Gospels are freely used, but Christ is everywhere presented in all the dignity and benignity and beauty of His true Character. The scenes of His life, trial and death are described with vividness as of a personal witness."

The American Hebrew
"...Not since "Ben-Hur: A Story of Christ," "Quo Vadis," the romance of Nero and the first Christian martyrs, has a book been written illuminating as

brightly the events of nineteen hundred years ago as does "The Sorry Tale." It is replete with descriptions and pictures of life in the Holy Land at the period described, and independently of the religious views the reader may hold it reads with tremendous interest, and, what is more, leaves in one's mind an indelible impression of spiritual beauty interwoven with the great tragedy of life."

William Reedy review in the St. Louis *Globe,* April 1, 1917
"...The plot is worked out with the precision of a Sardou, and its culmination is not discovered until the very end ... The conversations of Christ are beautiful in form and orthodox in spirit even where and when they depart farthest from the recorded words of Matthew, Mark, Luke and John. The scene in the garden of Gethsemane is an exquisite piece of writing, while the version of the trial and the crucifixion of Jesus is of a marvelous meticulosity of strange detail. ... The book is full of writing that biblical scholars call wisdom. It is beautiful and deep when one has mastered the difficulties of its form."

W. T. Allison, Author and Professor of English Literature, University of Manitoba
"...No book outside the Book of books gives such an intimate picture of the earthly life of Jesus, and no book has ever thrown such a clear light upon the manner of life of Jews and Romans in the Palestine of the day of our Lord ..."

Roland Greene Usher, Professor of History, Washington University
"...Certain adjectives come to me descriptive of the characters – cameo-like, vivid, dramatic. All are too weak to convey a sense of the startling definiteness

with which a man is invested with presence and reality in a line or even a phrase. There is a local color totally unlike that of the encyclopedia-crammed author of the usual novel of the Holy Land. ...The sheer beauty of the chapter on the Sermon on the Mount; the spirituality of the passage descriptive of the Last Supper and the evening at Gethsemane; the moving narrative of the last days, and the terrific climax of the Crucifixion, I shall not soon forget. Unquestionably this is the greatest story penned of the life and times of Christ since the Gospels were finished. One leaves it with a sense of understanding much previously dark and vague. Certainly I am myself practical and finite enough, brought up in the Doubting Thomas attitude of the modern school of historians; my own imagination is, I fear, none too sensitive and agile and that may be the explanation of my feeling that somehow she has contrived to make divinity plausible, convincing, adequate. Jesus as she depicts him seems divine to me, seems to act and speak as I feel He should ..."

The Rev. Joseph Fort Newton, pastor of The City Temple in London and rector of Memorial Church of St. Paul in Philadelphia.

"...Her story entitled The Sorry Tale is simply tremendous in its dramatic grasp and power. As a story of the time of Christ I do not know anything quite like it for sheer tragedy and spiritual beauty. The whole conception is striking and its execution is extraordinary... The pages, in particular, which tell of the Sermon on the Mount are not to be matched anywhere. As to how <Worth's books are> written, I make no question; I simply do not know. But I do bear testimony to their spiritual depth and their literary value. In these respects they are surely authentic."

Original Preface to *The Sorry Tale*
By Casper S. Yost

The story of the invisible author of *The Sorry Tale* was told in the book entitled *Patience Worth: a Psychic Mystery*. It seems sufficient here to present a brief statement of the facts in relation to that phenomenal personality. She came to Mrs. John H. Curran, of St. Louis, Missouri, one evening in the summer of 1913, as Mrs. Curran sat with a ouija board on her knees, and introduced herself as *Patience Worth*, with the declaration that she had lived long ago and now had come again. From that time she has poured out a continuous stream of communications, conversational or literary, including hundreds of poems, numerous parables and allegories, several short stories, a drama, and two novels. All of her compositions are distinguished by the archaic form of her language, which is, however, not the same in any two of her larger works, there being important dialectal variations that make each one quite different from the others in this particular, and the archaic quality as well as the dialectal form varies as much in her minor productions and in her conversations. Yet upon all of them is the impress of a single creative personality. Each and every one of them bears the imprint of Patience Worth.

Mrs. Curran, through whom all of this has come, is a young woman of normal disposition and temperament, intelligence and vivacious. She receives the communications with the aid of the mechanical device known as the ouija board as a recording instrument. There is no trance or any abnormal mental state. She sits down with the ouija board as she might sit down to a typewriter, and the receipt of the communications begins with no more ceremony than a typist would observe. Mrs. Curran has had no experience in literary composition and has made no study of literature, ancient or modern. Nor, it may be added, has she made any study of the history, the religions, or the social customs of the period of this story, nor of the geography or topography of the regions in which it is laid. Her knowledge of Palestine and of the beginnings of the Christian religion is no greater, and probably no less, than that of the average communicant.

Patience Worth began the writing of this story on the evening of the fourteenth of July, 1915, and some time was given to its transmission on two or three evenings of every week until its completion. In the early months she proceeded leisurely with the task, usually writing 300 to 1,000 words of the story in an evening, and, in addition, poems, parables, or didactic or humorous conversation, as the mood or the circumstances prompted. As a relief to the sorrows of *The Sorry Tale* she started another story which she called *The Merry Tale,* and for months the composition of the two stories continued alternately. Often she would work at both in the same evening. But as *The Sorry Tale* progressed she gave more and more time to it, producing on many evenings from 2,500 to 3,500 words of the tale in a sitting of an hour and a half or two hours. In one evening 5,000 words were dictated, covering the account of the Crucifixion. At all times, however, it came with great rapidity, taxing the chirographic speed of Mr. Curran to the utmost to put it down in abbreviated longhand. The nature of the language made it unsafe to attempt to record it stenographically. At the beginning of the story Patience had a little difficulty in dropping some of the archaic forms she had previously used, and which she continued to use in her other productions and in her conversations; but this difficulty seemed to disappear in a few weeks, and thereafter there was never a change of a word, never a pause in the transmission, never a hesitation in the choice of a word or framing of a sentence. The story seemed literally to pour out, and the amount of her production in an evening appeared to be limited only by the physical powers of Mrs. Curran. *Ye see*, she said once to a visitor who inquired about this ability to write with such pauseless continuity, *man setteth up his cup and filleth it, but I be as the stream.* As in all her work, it mattered not who was present or who sat at the board with Mrs. Curran. Whether the *vis-à-vis* was a man or woman, old or young, learned or unlettered, the speed and the quality of the production were the same. From start to finish some 260 persons contributed in this way to the composition of this strange tale, some helping to take but a few hundred words, some many thousands. Parts of the story were taken in New York, Boston and Washington. Each time the story was picked up at the point where work was stopped at the previous sitting, without a break in the continuity of the narrative, without the slightest hesitation, and without the necessity of a reference to the closing words of the last preceding installment. These words were often read for the benefit of those present, but Patience repeatedly proved that it was not required by her.

For some weeks before the beginning of the story Mrs. Curran had received intimations of its coming and of its nature: *'Tis sorry tale* (a tale of sorrow) *I put a-next*, Patience said on the fifth of July. *Aye, a lone-eat tale. Ye ne'er do to know an eat like to a lone. Be ye lone* (alone) *eat doth bitter.* It was as *the sorry tale* that she ever afterward spoke of it. On the evening of the ninth she entertained a company of twelve persons and in the midst of her conversation she exclaimed: *Hear ye a song!* and presented the following verses referring to this story and the material she desired for it:

> *Wind o' the days and nights,*
> *Aye, thou the searchers of the night,*
> *Lend thou to me of thee.*

Sun of the day, a-bath o'er Earth,
Lend thou of thee to me.

Rains of the storm,
A-wash of Earth's dust to a-naught,
Lend thou of thee to me.

Sweets o' the Earth, the glad o' day,
Lend thou of thee to me.

Prayers o' the soul, the heart's own breath,
Lend thou to me of thee.

Dark o' the nights, strip o' thy robe,
And lend o' thee to me.

For I do weave and wash and soothe
And cloak o' one who needeth thee,
A one o' His, a-stricken,
A one whose soul hath bathed o' crime,
And Earth hath turned and wagged a nay to him.

Two persons besides the Curran family – Mr. and Mrs. Curran and Mrs. Pollard, Mrs. Curran's mother – were present on the evening of July 14, two persons under whose hands Patience had expressed a wish to begin the tale. There was a certain solemnity to the occasion, a feeling that something of profound significance was to be inaugurated. Solemnity is quite unusual in the meetings with Patience, whose exuberant humor is one of her most charming qualities, and who, however serious she may be, loves not a long face. But on this night there were no flashes of wit. On the contrary, it was for a while a tremorous, hesitating, faltering Patience, almost overcome by the task upon which she was entering.

Loth, loth I be, she said. *Yea, thy handmaid's hands do tremble. Wait thou! Wait! Yet do I set* (to write). For a moment the pointer circled slowly about the board recording nothing until it picked up the murmur: *Loth, loth I be that I do for to set the grind* (the circling motion of the pointer). And then, for the first and only time in the long experience with her, she asked for a period of quiet. *Wait ye stilled*, she said. *Ah, thy handmaid's hands do tremble!*

For three or four minutes there was no sound in the room, and then, as if in reality from out the silence of twenty centuries, as if actually from out the darkness of the greatest night in all history came the plaintive cry of Theia, *Panda, Panda, tellest thou a truth?*

There was no further hesitation in the delivery. Without another pause, except by Mrs. Curran for rest and discussion, the story proceeded rapidly, and about two thousand words were received on that evening. The first thing noticed was the great difference in the language and the atmosphere from anything previously written by Patience. Next was the knowledge displayed of the people and the time and of the topography of the country. The language retained some of the verbal and syntactical peculiarities of Patience, the same freedom from grammatical restraints, but it was not the language of her other works, nor that which she used in her conversation. Her other productions of a narrative nature had been redolent of medieval or Renaissant England; the atmosphere of this was truly Syrian and Roman. But the knowledge shown was and is most puzzling. I do not undertake to say that there are no errors of fact or condition, no anachronisms. I merely assert that after much study and research I have been unable to find anything that I could so term with certainty. There are some things upon which no authority accessible to me gives any information. There are some variances from history, profane and sacred, but these are quite evidently intentional and with definite purpose. From the beginning to the end of the story Patience seemed to be absolutely sure of herself. Discussion of mooted points brought no comment from her and no modification of her statements. Several times she condescended to clear a doubt by later putting an explanation into the text, but in doing so she emphasized the original assertion. The interesting question arises: If Patience is, as she says, an Englishwoman of the seventeenth century, where did she get the knowledge and the material for this story? It is a question that gives rise to many speculations, but apparently she answered it for herself in the words of Theia to Tiberius in the Garden of the imperial palace at Rome: *'Thy hand did reach forth and leave fall a curtain of black that should leave a shadow ever upon the days of Theia. And the hand that shall draw the curtain wide and leave the light to fall upon thy shadows shall be this!'* – and she held her hand high.

    I have described the trepidation of Patience at the beginning of the story. Several times in the course of the composition she gave expression to this feeling, which seemed to grow out of a profound sense of personal responsibility. *Thee 'rt a-wind of a golden strand*, she said one evening. *This be the smile of Him that turneth back unto the past. The hand of thy handmaid shaketh at the task. This lyre singeth the song of Him. Think ye the hand of me might touch athout* (without) *a shake? 'Tis a prayer I'd put that the very shaking of this hand should cause a throbbing of the air of Heaven and set aflow the song unto the Earth.* And at another time she said: *This holied tale be the love of me. Yet 'tis a sorry put* (a work of sorrow), *for woe is me that I do tell of the woes of Him*. Again she remarked, by way of introduction to an evening's work: *Athin* (within) *the put* (the story) *be much of Him, and this tale be dear unto me. Ye see, I be at put* (at the writing) *as though 'twere me upon thy earth. Yea, for how may a one tell unto his brother that that he knoweth as the dear wish of him unless he be as the brother of the flesh of him?* And then, further to voice her feelings, she gave this poem on Jesus by the Sea:

> *Calm eyes a-look 'cross sea.*
> *The seething waters lap 'pon sands*
> *At feet of Him. The day a-bathed of blood,*
> *A-sounded 'mid the soothing of the sea's*
> *soft voice.*
> *Earth, old, olden, yea,*
> *And yet so youthed, so youthed!*
> *And He a-sit, calm-eyed, years youthed,*
> *And wisdom olded past the tell.*
>
> *And lo, His voice a-mingled there*
> *With silver tongues of speaking waves.*
> *The rolling waters lapped*
> *The very murmur of His prayer.*
> *And e'en this day, methinks,*
> *'Tis tongued unto the earth.*
>
> *The sand's soft clung about the feet a-bared*
> *That still should trod 'pon stones a-sharped.*
> *Yea, Earth e'en then did hold the greened*
> *tree*
> *That burst the sod for upping of the cross.*
>
> *And lo, the voices of the Earth*
> *Cried out and sounded discord*
> *'Mid the heaven-song of Him.*
> *And He a-walked Him from the sea's calm*
> *shore*
> *And through the vale, the bitter cup to sup.*

> *Methinks that there within the garden place*
> *I see me of His holied self a-stripped.*
> *No brother of the flesh might know of Him,*
> *For God be God and man doth fear to know.*
> *And Earth doth stand it, still a-crying out*
> *Against this song of love.*
> *And yet, I do to see Him sit,*
> *Calm eyes unto the sea*
> *And wisdom past the tell.*

Upon still another evening she said: *Look ye! The side that flowed red doth weep fresh drops, e'en unto this day. Yea aday! And this shed of the tides* (times) *agone but bought of the then, and yet He, smiling, sheddeth ever, yea, ever. The every day seeth the weeped drops. Think ye then that this hand would set these drops gushed, or yet touch them that fell and be dust that they stir in their holy, athout* (without) *a tremor?*

Ah, men of Earth, look! look! Amid thy day stalketh He. Yea, and thou mayest see His drops aflow e'en upon thy byways. Yea, and what doest thou that the drops be stopped? He be the oped chalice that poureth the cleansed flow ever, ever, ever. Think ye that they who fall, bathed of blood, be stopped athin (within) *their own flow? Nay! – born anew athin* (within) *His own. Yea, His arms cradles seas. Yea, and His hands plucketh e'en the motes as His own. Yea, His treasures gleam. And I be a-telling thee-ah, joy!-much be His that He doth treasure that Earth hath cast as chaff. E'en though His vineyard showeth blight, still within His press, behold, naught save sweeted wines do flow!*

I presented these expressions of profound devotion to show the sentiment that has unquestionably actuated Patience Worth in the production of this story. There is much within it to arouse discussion, but she has no fear. *Hark ye!* she says. *There shall be ones who shall tear at this cloth till it shreddeth, yet the shreds shall weave them back unto the whole 'pon love strands. For love be the magic warp, and Love may ne'er die, but be born athin all hearts that sup the words.*

C. S. Y.

OPINION OF CLEMENT WOOD[1]

Mr. Wood, a graduate of the University of Alabama and of the Yale Law School, is author of many novels and volumes of verse, also a short story writer for various magazines. In the New York *Call*, August 26, 1917, he names *The Sorry Tale* "The Gospel According to Patience," and declares that "it is worthy to be called this." He pronounces the passage "Unto thee do I deliver the watchword of the Kingdom – Mercy. Unto thee do I deliver the Key – Faith. Unto thee do I deliver the Kingdom – Love" as "a little gem" and adds: "This is as exquisite as Corinthians 13, the loveliest part of the New Testament." While in his opinion the book would be improved if much shortened, still he says: "But it is a wonderful book."

---

[1] Reprinted from *The Case of Patience Worth* by Franklin Prince, University Books, Inc., 1964

EDITOR'S NOTES

The main text for *The Gospel of Jesus Christus According To Patience Worth* was extracted word for word from the book *The Sorry Tale: A Story Of The Time Of Christ*. The editor parsed the text into chapters and provided chapter headings – the chapter headings are NOT part of the original text. Footnotes denoted by symbols are found in the original text. Footnotes denoted by numbers are new and provide context or background information.

He was in the world,
And though the world was made through him,
The world did not recognize him.
He came to that which was his own,
But his own did not receive him.

John 1:10-11 (NIV)

The Gospel of Jesus Christus
According to Patience Worth

Jesus Is Born

1. "The babe town[1] is full, o'erfull of wonders this dawning. Shepherds came with wonder-tidings and told of the star that shewed and trailed a beard like a priest's beard, long and bright. Ha, ha! They searched the highways and byways and sought a babe. A woman, a traveler, and one Joseph, bedded in a manger, and she, named Mary, was with child and delivered there. And they sought and found the babe, and they tell of a vision of bright ones that sang and spake unto them. And they kneeled, and spiced the garments of her who bore the babe and kissed the hem of the swaddling-cloth. And they made obeisance and spake that o'er the sleeping babe and mother a light shewed like unto golden cloth."

Mary Offers Up the Doves

2. And Theia[2] and Panda[3] and Simeon[4] bided them within the house of Flavius[5] until the time when Mary should bring forth the Babe unto the temple and offer up the doves unto the priests.

And they set them, upon this day, upon the path unto the temple, and they waited at the wall's ope until Joseph and Mary should enter therein.

And lo, they came them. And Mary was seated upon an ass, and Joseph walked him beside, and Mary held close the Babe wrapped of cloth; and Joseph carried a basket of woven reed wherein the doves were put. Then went they unto the temple.

---

[1] Bethlehem
[2] Hatte's mother
[3] Theia's slave
[4] Former Roman gladiator
[5] A Roman senator and nobleman

And Mary stepped from off the ass, and the head of her was high. Yea, and she held the Babe aloft. And they made them their ways within, nor knew they them who followed. And the way was darkened until the time, and lo, the sun broke forth and showed upon the Babe and she who bore Him.

And the woman Anna rose and came forth and spake: "This is the Christ!"

And the priest spake them: "Yea, this is the seed of Abraham. This is He of whom the scripts foretold."

And the eyes of Mary looked on high, and the face of her told not of that which abided in the heart of her. And the priests marveled at this woman, that she had born the seed of David and yet looked not upon herself with pride. For Mary spake no word, but kept within her heart much.

Herod's Wrath Waxes

3. And Herod made much word unto the high priests, and called council with the scribes. And they spake that the scripts had foretold of the coming of this governor from out the land of Judea.

And Herod gnashed his teeth, and rent his robes, and said that the hand of him would smite the firstborn of the land. Yea, and he heard much of the coming of these men who rode them from afar; for they did ask of him: "Where is He who is born King of the Jews?"

And Herod held close unto his heart these words they spake, and said unto them: "Go thou and seek this child, that I may go forth and worship."

And within his heart he held much evil, for Herod held naught but the undoing as the right for this King. Then set he forth and lo, the lands of Judea shook with wailing, for Herod plucked forth love from out the arms of women, for their babes were the root of love.

And there were murmurings that set upon the land of Jerusalem of this King that was born, and after the slaying they that did remain were in fear of Herod. And no man sought to come within the walls lest Herod hear of the flesh of him and slay it.

Several Years Later, an Account of Jesus, Who Now Lives in Nazareth

4. And Paul[1] spake slow: "Panda, there cometh word from out Nazareth of a one who worketh Him 'mid woods and speaketh words that no man knoweth.[•] Yea, at the market's place, e'en this morn's hour, a one rode him upon a camel from out this land and spoke of this one and told of ones of Nazareth who had sought Him out and e'en though He shewed as a lad of young years the aged scribes sought Him and bade that He speak unto them."

And Panda spake: "What then doth Nazareth speak as the name that He beareth?"

And Paul answered: "Jesus," and told of the word among the people of visions and wisdoms. And Panda looked unto Paul and spake: "And thou hast spoken His name Jesus?"

And Paul made answering: "Yea," and told more; that among the Nazarenes who sought the one, abided many who knew the words He spoke and brought them forth unto Jerusalem, and these ones said that this Jesus spake not as the temple's men, but of sands and leaves, and made mighty walls of sand's grains, and forests deep of leaves.

And he told that among these men were two brothers who had of a flock, each one the half. And lo, smite[∝] fell upon the one half of the flocks and the brothers fell wrathed one against the other that the half that shewed smite should be set unto the half and that the half that shewed whole be set unto the half. For lo, the one spake that the sick half

---

[1] A minor character in the story of Hatte; not to be confused with the Apostle Paul
[•] Beyond their understanding
[∝] Sickness

was that of his brother and the whole his own. And they set each upon the other's flesh.°

And Nazareth saw this thing and bade that they seek this Jesus and tell Him of this.

And they sought Him out and lo, He stood at the stripping of barks from off the woods. And they spake unto Him, and lo, He lifted not His eyes. And they cried out unto Him: "What! Listeth thou not unto thy brother's woe?"

And He made answering: "Yea, mine ear harketh, yet followeth this hand the Father's bidding."

And they told unto Him of the flocks and raised their voices one 'gainst the other. And He looked not upon them but left their words that they mingle in wrathing.

And they cried aloud, and He harkened but turned not.

And the brothers wearied of their wrath and spake one unto the other of the whole ones of the flocks, and shewed one unto the other that these scattered upon the fields e'en as they warred.

And they spake soft and sought more of the words of Jesus, and lo, He stopped and lay the woods by.

And they told that the airs spread forth His locks and His mantle blew and wrapped Him 'bout. And He raised up His hands and looked unto the fields and spake: "Call thee unto thy sheep."

And they raised their voices and cried out the sheep's call, and lo, the sheep came unto them and hung 'bout their limbs. And Jesus oped up His arms and shewed this thing unto them and spake: "Seest thou? Sheep know not one brother from the other. Go thou and do likewise; for lo, doth the sheep's lead go unto the rutted places, even so the flock.

Alike them, thou sons of man, seek thee the fields and know ye one sheep be like unto another; even so men."

° Came to blows

And they looked upon Him and He took up a lamb and held it unto Him and spake: "Even as lambs come unto the fold and the shepherd ministereth unto them, so cometh woe unto thy brothers. Do thou then but turn the shepherd's staff unto the days of man, for lo, thy brother needeth not more of thy ministering than one of these, doest thou this in loving."

And they raised up their voices and spake: "Tell unto us of the wisdom, and where in the fields and the days of Nazareth a man may find wisdom and know wisdom."

And lo, He took up a bit of stone and dropped this within the pool, and spake: "When man knoweth the all of this, man hath wisdom. Yea, for wisdom, like unto this stone's path, swalloweth up even its own course."

Jesus Takes Up the Staff

5. And within Nazareth morn broke.

The hills lay wrapped of rose; the sky's mantle shewed deck of stars and hung of white fleece; the vineyards glisted of gems and the sweet airs stirred the deep-grown fields; and the sheep lay not yet waked.

And behold, a one came Him forth and trod the hill's path even so that the sun that came forth o'er the brow shewed Him radiant.

And He stretched forth His hands and called soft, and the sheep arose and came unto Him.

And He sat Him down and looked Him far, even o'er the ways that shewed from the high summit. And the lights shewed Him smiling unto the far.

And His feet were bared, and His mantle wet of young dew, and His eyes deep, deep blue, even as the sky, the sign of the might of God. And His locks flamed within the light and hung long and o'er His stooped shoulders. And the brow gleamed stained of the sun's heat, and His thin beard hid not the sweet that clung His lips. And lo, when He raised His hand, it was even as the soft skimming of a swallow's wing.

And the sun kissed the bended back whereon earth's woes should rest; and the grasses lay soft 'gainst His feet and even clung.

And He stretched forth His hands and looked upon them, and behold, upon the flesh shewed the stain of the staff. And He looked upon this and smiled, and took up a staff of broken wood that lay, and spake: "The Son of Man shall fashion out His staff,[*] that they know."

And He arose and sought the valley; and the sheep followed, and the road's-ways swallowed their going.

Jesus Drinks Old Wine Out of New Cups
6. And Hezekiah[1] spake: "No man knoweth deeper wisdom than this Jesus. Yea, His cunning hath turned the words of the prophets and He hath drunk the old wines from out of new cups. Out of Egypt hath come ones who have sought that they see this one who hath caused the shaking of Herod[∝] upon his throne; for even though Herod knoweth not, and the blood of Herod knoweth not, this young Jew is that that hath caused the throne's quaking. And these men are wise ones who know the prophets of all ages, and this lad suppeth their wine-skins dry. Yea, their words He speaketh, their scripts He knoweth, their wisdoms He sheareth as sheep and keepeth the wools. And one among them hath lended unto Him all his knowing, and behold, He hath taken not the lending but the keeping of it. And no man asketh He of an aid. Even when famine hath set He feareth not. When all men cry out He smiles."

---
[*] The Son of Man shall so shape His life that the world shall understand its purpose.
[1] A minor character in the story of Hatte
[∝] Herod Antipas, tetrarch of Galilee

Rome's Men Tempt Jesus

7. And at the morn, from out the household of one Isicher, came forth two brothers, and their robes shewed them of Rome. And they sought the hill's-ways and the sheep's places, and came upon the shepherds at their tending and spake words unto them and asked if the hands of this Jew, Jesus, had wrought witcheries. And the shepherds said that this was against the prophet's word. And the Rome's ones spake: "Yea, but word goeth forth that He hath done this thing."

And they sought them on. And behold, they came upon Him, Jesus, the sheep's tender. And His sheep stood within the valley while He sat Him high, bowed o'er a script of skin.

And his ears took not in their coming. And they came up unto Him and spake words, saying: "Art thou Jesus?"

And He spake Him "yea," and His eyes shewed unto them the depth of peace. And they said: "'Tis spoken that thou art the Son of God, the King of Promise unto the Jews."

And He called unto his sheep and spake not. And they made more of words, saying: "If this saying is true, cast thee down, for thy Sire shall take thee up."

And He looked not upon them but spake of sheep. And they shewed unto Him gold and rare stuffs, and said: "Shouldst thou cast thee down, this is thine."

And He spake not.

And they said: "If this is thine, thy brothers shall fall down and worship thee."

And He held His hands high unto the coming sun and spake: "It is written that no man shall worship save one God."

And they said: "But thou shouldst be a man among men."

And He spake: "Nay, nay, but a shepherd among sheep."

And they pointed unto lands and leaned close and whispered: "The mighty one could minister unto thee even a kingdom."

And His lips smiled the smile of a father's sorrow o'er youth's folly. And He stretched forth His arms unto their utmost and spake: "Behold thou the sky! Behold thou the lands! Behold thou the kingdoms of the earth, and all men! These are the heritage of the Son of Man and the goods of my Father."

And they laughed in mockery and spake words of scorning and made them more of words, telling of that that should fall unto His day should He cast Him down and know not the Jews as His brothers. And He spake: "Get thee behind me, evil ones! I will not of thee!"

And He took up His staff and walked unto His sheep and spake no word more, even though they followed Him on the way.

Paul's Witness to the Teachings of Jesus
8. And Abraham listed and rubbed his knees and Isaac made on, saying: "Paul knoweth much, Abraham. He bore word for Levi and hath returned with much word from out Nazareth of this Jesus. He sayeth that within the synagogue He ariseth and readeth out the scripts and the words each seem a score and that that confoundeth cleareth as salted water. He hath spoken unto the people even within the streets. It is said that they follow Him and come unto Him with their woes and hopes. And unto them that speak out unto Him but believe not in their hearts He sayeth, 'Shew thou thyself unto the priests.'

"And they seek Him and tell unto His ears that there are some in Nazareth that would not of Him. And He sayeth unto them that a man might root within the land that bore him but He should branch upon the far places and blossom farther still.

"He troubleth not o'er that that troubleth men and woeth o'er that that woeth not man. When a man's flesh falleth fevered do they call upon His aid He goeth thereto and doth He find the fever cometh out of the o'erladen spirit – hath the man done wrongly and suffereth the hot of shame – 'tis told that He ministereth unto him. And be it this thing, He freeth his spirit of the pack, and behold, the fever falleth low. But be it but flesh, He careth little.

"He hath spoken that there be two things that befalleth a man that setteth his flesh sick: he hath sinned, or his flesh hath worn it o'er labor or time's bite. He hath said that sinning setteth up flesh-rot[*] and is not of His Father's handiwork. The body, He hath told, is a vessel, and doth a man put within his vessel that that it be not fashioned for to hold, he suredly shall wear it or yet break it.

"Yea, and He hath told that did not sin write upon a man's flesh, and the writing hurt sore, he would fall short of his days; for his vessel would never hold. In these words hath He told that unto a man a bowl is but a bowl, and a scar upon it but a scar and yet a break but a break; for he may take him a new bowl. But his body crieth out at his own sinning. This is the chiding, for He speaketh that doth a man heed the crying out, his vessel will last. And this is within the hand of man and not the hand of His Father.

"Yet there be men that write upon their flesh so deep that it floweth within the blood of their kind. And this man is an abomination and shall be called that he wipe out the scripts he hath writ. Doth his flesh come forth empty, as a fool, through his sinning, then he shall fill their empty, even though 'tis within a new day.

"His Father's land, He hath told, Abraham, is a land where thou art dealt fully unto. He that is empty shall be filled, for the empty ones be the flowers of the full-dealt tree. Man is like unto a tree, and his blood floweth out unto

---

[*] Disease

the last small bud, and even though this bud leaf not, it holdeth that that maketh the leaf and shall burst unto a leaf. He hath spoken this, Abraham. Is it not wisdom?

"And He hath spoken more: that the scripts upon earth are the shadows of wisdom, yet man seeth wisdom within the scripts. Writ words make no sound, yet loud noises. Out of the shadows which are scripts man plucketh him a thing that is his. Nor doth he pluck it off the scripts, for his brother may pluck, and his brother's brother, and take unto them.

"Of such is the wisdom of heaven, He hath told, for it is the thing that hangeth upon the scripts and maketh them bottomless pits of wisdom."

A Tempest Arises from an Ant Hill

9. And they passed, upon the way, men who sought the greens with their beasts, and they made the sign of morning unto these. And behold, they looked unto Hassan, whose robe shewed him not of their land, and bended low, even unto their back's bendings. And it was true they came upon Hezekiah who sought the hut of Panda, and they worded with him at the road's side. And Hezekiah told of much that filled the days of Nazareth, for from out an ant's hill had arisen a tempest. And Hassan asked of Jesus Christus, and Hezekiah answered that He had been within Galilee, within the synagogues, and had spoken among their holy men, and had returned unto Nazareth and gone within the synagogue and spoken unto the people. Yea, He had oped the scripts and sought a spot prophet-tongued. And He had arisen up among them and spoken that the prophet's words were fulfilled, for He had come that He feed unto the earth the bread of God. And they had spoken unto Him, saying: "Then call thee unto the rich men and bid that they come forth and give freely unto the poor, for we are hungered and Nazareth is filled of but poor. Since thou art come, do this thing."

And He had arisen, Hezekiah spake, unto a high place whereon the priests stood, and had spread His hands forth and looked Him unto the people and His eyes glisted of tears and He spake: "I am come to make whole the broken, to bind up the broken-hearted, to soothe the bruised, to dry up weeping, to make of emptiness fullness. The bread of God shall I deliver unto them that hunger. I am come to minister unto the poor, be this the poor who have little of earth's wares or he whose spirit is barren. He that is full needeth me not. Thou wilt speak unto me: 'If thou art a healer, heal thine own sores. Physician heal thyself.' And I shall answer thee: 'He who delivereth the bread of God unto His people is healed. Through each crumb is he purged. Look! Among ye it is spoken, 'Is not this the son of Joseph?' I speak unto ye, a prophet may not be lifted up among his own people.[*]

"Look ye unto it. In the days of Israel, in the time when the heavens shut and famine came upon them, unto but one came there the sign. This is the sign. There may be but one who be the Father's Son; yet all of ye are His sons. Even so hath He begat me within His own love and brought me out of the earth a living sign unto man that He entereth all men."

And it had been true that the men had wrathed o'er this and spake that He set Him up o'er them and had spoken that He should go forth. Even with loud noises had they broken the worship. And it was true that Jesus had gone from their midst.

And Hezekiah told that He had gone unto Capernaum and had preached among them and they had listed unto Him, but at one morn when He had gathered together a band that they worship beneath the sun, a man had arisen and spoken aloud unto Him: "Who art thou that shouldst

---

[*] Luke 4

use the tongue of the priests? What have we to do with thee?"

And Jesus had spoken unto him, saying: "This evil is upon thy tongue and cometh forth."

And the man had spoken not, but stood and listed unto the words of Jesus unto the band of worshipers. And behold, this man had been known as one who was wicked and filled of the evil one. And when the words of Jesus Christus had ceased, behold, he fell upon his knees and cried out: "I know thee. Thou art the Son of God!" And he had gone upon his way a new man.

And Hezekiah told that they that had seen this spake unto Jesus, saying: "Thou hast driven forth the devil within him; for this man hath bitten the airs in wickeds and made sounds even as the swine."

And it was true that Jesus had spoken that a man's evil might not be driven forth, but should the man sup of the living waters, behold, the evils might drown. "This is before thee and thou mayest speak it, but the days shall come when this shall rust and man know but the rust's crust. But the might of God shall touch the crumble of rust, and behold, the truth shall be upon thee!

"I am fulled and thou art empty, yet should I fill thee thou wouldst burst. Yet my words shall I pin unto the tongues of men through ages, that they shall speak His name."

The Netting of Fish

10. And at the morn's coming there shewed upon the out-roads Jesus Christus, and within His hands shewed a blade such as a wood's man[*] plied. And He sought the out-ways unto a city's place wherein He should wield this thing and bring forth bread. And behold, He came upon a man whose

---

[*] A carpenter

head was bowed and He spake Him, saying: "Whither goest thou?"

And the man made answering: "I seek Nazareth from out Gennesareth way. They that have sent me forth hunger that He come unto them, this man that dealeth the bread of words wherefrom men may eat. He is called Jesus Christus. They have sent unto Him of their goods," and the man drew forth a sack of moneys, "that He know they would of Him."

And lo, Jesus Christus touched not the skin's-sack and spake: "I go unto these who hunger, for I am Him, Jesus Christus. But no man hath goods that may purchase the bread of life. This do I minister freely, even as He that sent me ministereth rains, dews and sweet airs."

And the man sunk upon his knees and spake soft: "Master."

And Jesus said unto him: "Arise. I am but a shepherd and no man's master." And He spake: "I would seek, following thee, unto this spot where the hungered wait."

And when they had come unto the town's place, which was a babe town upon a shore's rise, behold, no man looked them welcome. And he that had come unto Nazareth spake: "They that have sent me forth await yon."

And he pointed unto a thick of boats that loved the shore, and he said: "Within this spot there is no temple and the holy places would be shut unto thee. Master, we may but offer unto thee these that the people may hark," and he pointed unto the boats.

And Jesus Christus stood upon the shore and looked afar and spake: "It is well. Look ye! Is not this a fitting holy spot? Boundless the sea's wave and the sky's arch. It is well. Come thou! We shall put the words within the boats that they float whither and seek new lands."

And they drew nigh where there stood upon the shore them that waited. And Jesus spake word of greeting unto them by the flashing of His sweet smile. And they cried aloud: "We hunger! Thy words tear down the stone walls and leave us in."

And it was true that He stood among them and spake: "Busy thee at thy tasks, for the words I bring are for busied men."

And they whose boats stood sought them, and among them washed nets and made right for the going out. And amid the sweet notes of the voice that spake gentleness unto them sounded the lapping of the waters and the stirring of the waves about the boats by the washing of nets.

And upon the shore's-way rested them that would hark, and they spake unto Jesus Christus, saying: "What may we offer thee? For look! There is no spot where thou mayest rest and thou hast trodden far. Even the dusts of the road cling to thee and weariness is thine."

And He made answer: "Draw thee yon boat up unto the water's edge and therein shall I rest and speak with thee, and ye shall sit even upon the shores and hark, so that when words shall cease thou mayest hear the sea's wisdom."

And they brought forth the boat and made it to rest upon the shallow waters. And He walked Him unto it, and there followed, even within the waters, ones who would be near Him. And they spake: "'Tis spoken that thou hast the key that unlocketh the temples."

And He answered them, saying: "No key may unlock the temple, for within it abideth not the God. For man hath his God even as he hath his shadow. The prophets have spoke and told thee of the wraths. Behold, He hath sent a new tongue for to tell of mercies."

And they made silence before this thing and the hands busied at their tasks. And they that harked upon the shores sat them long waiting, and one who sat within the boat, even beside Him, spake: "Master, tell unto us, for we are wicked. Yea, our deeds fall short and love abideth not among us."

And He spake Him, saying: "Behold, there may not be an earth save for love. The sky boweth down in loving unto the earth. The stars send reaching beams unto the earth. The moon leadeth the waters from one shore unto the other in loving. The sun sheddeth him o'er all things in loving. Behold, there be not e'en a flying bird whose shadow traileth him not. And this is the sign of love. Ye may not know the depth of love, save that thou lookest unto thine own shadow; for a man may not measure love save that he deal it, and looketh unto himself even so that he knoweth his shadow's tracking."

And they spake: "We know not thy words. Speak unto us within that[∝] we know."

And He stood Him up within the boat and took up a net and left it hang within His hands, and said: "Thou dost hark unto these things, and behold, the nets lie them idle."

And they spake: "But we have wearied, for the casting bringeth forth naught. Behold, look upon this morn's netting even at thy feet, scarce a score."

And He said: "Put thee off the shore and cast."

And they murmured: "Nay, 'tis vain; for the nets have been spread therein and brought forth naught. How then may we bring forth fish from out the shallow places?"

And He answered them, saying: "I speak unto thee in that thou knowest. Put thee off the shore and cast."

And upon the shore arose the voices, speaking out: "This man is wise! Do thou this thing!"

And the men whose boat He stood within made ready. And He stood even as the boat started off the shallows, and lights gleamed upon His locks, and His mantle of coarse stuffs hung soft unto Him, and His lips moved. And all who listed stood mute before the spell of the music of His voice.

[∝] Within our capacity to understand

And the boat slipped unto the waters off the shallows. And they watched, and behold, He bade that the nets be spread and let fall. And behold, Simon the fisher let down the nets but his words spake: "Why dost thou bid that we fish in the fished waters? It is vain."

And Jesus made answering: "Dost thou leave thy net down in no faith how may it find aught save thy folly?"

And He caused that Simon bring up the net. And Simon fell upon his face and cried out: "I am a wicked man! Behold, before thee have I set my doubt. Aye, and how may a man's doubt become greater than his God, save that he put his doubt before his God?"

And Jesus said: "Thou hast acknowledged thy doubt and fallen down before it. Cast thou the nets!"

And Simon let fall the net unto the waters, and behold the waters stirred and the boats swayed, even so that it seemed that storms lay beneath the water. And they made to draw forth the nets, and behold, the fish leaped high and the silver shewed glisted within the light. And within the boat the men were not enough that they draw forth the nets. And they that watched saw, and men sprang unto the waters and swam to the spot and lended aid that they bring forth the nets. And they marveled and said: "What is this man?" And they cried: "Master! Master!"

And behold, their voices arose unto a tumult as they brought the nets back unto the shores, and men swam with the boat and held unto the nets that they bring forth the catch. And when they had come unto the shore and the boat lay within the shallows Jesus called forth unto all of them and delivered the fish unto them. And they cried: "This is wondrous! What is it?"

And Jesus made answer: "This is naught. For the netting of fish is little unto the bringing forth of men."

And Simon fell upon his face and spake unto Him of his wickedness. And Jesus said: "Arise and put thy nets by; for thou shalt weave a net of thy love and bring forth men."

And they spake: "It shall be; for this man hath looked unto lands and even though his nets slipped the waters his dreaming was not there."

And they spake unto Him more, saying: "It hath come that thou hast lain low fever and hath cleansed and healed. What is that that is thine that is no man's?"

And He answered: "The time is not come that thou shalt know, but it is true that no man will hark save that a loud noise setteth up. Thou mayest not know, but within thy land the eyes shall ope and the ears hark, unto the eye's undoing and the confounding of the ears."

Jesus Deals the Living Bread

11. And it was true that within a certain city multitudes had followed the footfalls of Jesus, and cried out unto Him that He fill them up. And He had come unto them with them that He had chosen for to be His brothers* and deal the living bread. And they wearied, for there was no spot whose walls were so wide that they might take in the multitudes. And these were beggars, publicans, sinners, aye, and Jews. Even them of other lands came unto Him that they hark. Thereby He wove of all men His footcloth.

And they that He called His brothers spake unto Him, saying: "Master, shew unto us how it is that the bread should be offered."

And He answered them, saying: "Yon, upon the mount, 'tis shaded. Come! Bring forth them that would list, and seek the spot. Out of the city's places, away from all that that setteth din, come, and the bread shall be thine."

And they followed Him, but He spake: "Nay; go ye before! For the ages have preceded the Son of Man. Thereby He is even as the shepherd."

And they spake one unto the other, saying: "See ye, He putteth Him not up and o'er us. Behold, are we not the

---

* His disciples

footcloths for all men? Do not our brothers trod upon us, and the priests hide the God?"

And they went up into the mount. And they waited the coming of Jesus. Even did they part unto the halving and leave Him through that He seek a high spot from where to speak unto them. And the brothers that He knew followed Him and spake: "Master, shew unto us the ministering of the bread."[∞] And He made answer: "He may not feed a multitude. Nay, but break thou one bit for the feeding of one and another for the feeding of another."

And they said: "How then may we make words that we may feed every man? For suredly, do we cast the bread wide, some may fatten and others shall hunger."

And He spake: "He who ministereth shall touch that that he ministereth unto. The Father is with thee even as with me. Unto all men He is *the* God.[x] Unto one man He is *the* God. Unto all men He is the Father, but unto every man is He sire."

And they said: "How dost thou speak this? We take it not in."

And He spake: "Bring forth thy brothers, one, then the other, that we feed."

And they brought forth a one whose body was covered not save of rag-cloth, deep-dyed of dusts, whose skin had shrunk and left his bones writ upon it. And they said: "Master, behold this man is a beggar. What manner of bread hast thou for him?"

And Jesus leaned unto him and took up his hand and spake: "Cast thy staff! Thou needest it not, for thou hast bread. Blessed is he who hath not, for it shall be given unto him."

[∞] The word
[x] The italicized words in this and following utterances of Jesus are so emphasized at the direction of P. W.

And He stood, holding the beggar's hand, and spake unto them: "Look ye; he hath not, but his day is thine, his water is thy sup, his breath is even as thine. The road's-ways that bear thee are his. His day is filled not of the changing and barting; thereby he is empty of goods of earth and may be filled up." And He said unto the beggar: "Even as thou art empty, even so shall it be given unto thee."

And lo, the beggar stood him up and cried out: "Master, it is true! Think ye!" – and he turned unto the multitude, - "my Sire cast yon ball! The bread is mine! Lo, out from Rome hath the noble blood° been cast within a crooked bowl,⊕ for to be filled up of precious stuffs!"

And they looked upon the beggar and saw the light within his eyes and knew his words as truth.

And they brought forth another, and he fell upon his face and spake: "Lord, I am unworthy of such a God as thou bringest. I am lowly and not the son of one even so high as yon beggar. I am the dusts of the road's-way. I am un-needful unto the earth."

And Jesus bid that he arise, and He smiled and lay His arm about the one and spake, smiling: "Blessed are the meek, for inasmuch as they cast them down they shall be lifted up."

And He smiled unto the down-cast eye of the one who had come unto Him and took him unto His breast, and turned His peace-filled eyes unto the multitude and then unto His loved ones, His brothers, and smiled and whispered soft: "Blessed are the meek, for they shall inherit the earth. All men shall list unto a brother who casteth him down. Yea, meekness buyeth love, and love hath the power for to buy the earth. Behold, a man whose raiment is beauteous, and filleth up the eye of his brother, o'er-cometh him. Yea, and the doors of the humble shall be closed unto

---

° One of noble blood
⊕ A hunchback

him. But he who is clothed within the cloth of meekness, goeth into the door of the mansion or yet into the hut's place; thereby no door is shut unto him. The door's-way unto the house of meekness is oped wide, and shut unto no thing. Thereby he who abideth within it knoweth all men as his brothers. He becometh as the dust of the road's-way, even unfit within his own eye to claim of the Father. He is empty, save of his fullness of the greatness of his Sire. Thereby is he full. Meekness is not the cloak of the hypocrite, but the armor of a Son of Man. Meekness casteth its eyes down but unto the might of the Father. Blessed are the meek."

And the one, who stood looking deep into the sweet eyes, sunk upon the bosom of Him and wept. And He took him unto Him close and spake: "It is well. Thou hast eaten the bread."

And the one answered: "Yea, and I am full."

And the multitudes stood before Him and their eyes glisted, and they pressed them closer; even did some among them sink upon their knees and speak prayers. And He turned unto the loved ones and said: "Bring forth thy brothers that they eat."

And afar the sounds of the city's day crept soft like an echo, and the trees that shaded, bended, swaying soft, and the ways spilled forth the singing of the winged hosts, and the bleating of sheep and the pipe of the shepherds came like the ghosts of some past day.

And His loved fell down before Him and murmured: "Lord!"

And He answered: "Arise! They hunger, and are not fed."

And they brought forth a one who came up unto the spot, crying out: "Behold, the days are empty! How may a man know the Sire, the Father? Behold, the sacrifices are but meat and feed us not. The bread that we eat within the temple hath not salt. Before the face of God they draw the holy veil. Yea, and fill up the temple with smoke, even so that no light may come unto us that we may see Him. The first-fruits are brought forth unto the priests, who eat it in His name. Thereby are they fed – and we hunger. This is not the Father thou tellest of, who would eat the grain of His son and respond not with His love. How may a man know the Father?"

And Jesus held forth His hand and took within it the hand of him who sought. And He turned unto the multitude and said: "Behold, this man is one of ye, for he hath set upon his tongue the thing that hath bidden ye hence." And He spake, and His lips smiled: "Blessed are the hungered, for they shall be filled."

And the multitude cried out: "Lord! Lord! We would bow down unto thee, yea, and worship thee!"

And He held His hands high and spake: "Nay! A man's worship is His labor. It is true that no thing is done in His name by him whose hands are idle. Would ye then worship, be ye at His labors. How might ye love me, yea, or yet know me as thy brother in the Father, save that I be thy brother in the flesh? And do I bear thee words from the Father, then shall I come as thy brother, since thy Sire is mine. Nor shall the words pour forth like beauteous streams to flow about the hill's-ways of earth and be forgot; but as bread, that no crumb shall be lost, and fed unto thee with *these hands,* that ye know thy Father's bread was dealt by thy brother, in loving and in the knowledge of thy hunger."

And He turned unto His loved ones and spake: "Behold, these are the Father's hungered. Thou art delivered His bread that thou mayest minister it. Become as thy brother, not o'er him, save as thou mayest be fuller of the Father. Then hark ye! Take out of thy fullness and lend unto thy brother."

And He chided them, saying: "Dost thou minister unto a beggar, make the bread beauteous, for his days are barren and he eateth crusts. And dost thou deal the bread unto him that is rich, strip ye it unto but the bread and minister it unto him, for it is well that he eat crusts. Bring ye the beggars that they kneel before the Father beside the rich. Robe them both in one cloth, the love of the Father. Take ye the rugs from out the temple that the beggars bed. Put ye not unto an altar His stuffs; for He hath builded the earth's day as His altar. Behold, the temple teems of gold; even do they bart upon her steps. The chalices of office° are of precious stuffs, filled with the blood of the first-fruits, when behold, the tears of babe's faces do dry upon the mother's breast and the mother hungereth, yea, looketh unto emptiness to find the Father of her day. The brightness that the Father looketh upon is not builded up of earth's precious stuff, but lieth within the heart of man. Thy riches are but the dusts of heaven. Blessed are the hungered for they are offered unto thee by the Father that thou mayest fill them. They are the golden chalices of office unto Him."

And they that harked marveled; for this spake against the temple. And He, looking upon them, perceived their marveling and smiled and said: "Even though man doeth this folly, the Father forgiveth him; for in their blindness they build of that that earth offereth unto the eye; yet, in the storing unto the Father of earth's dross, they fall them short of their filling and leave the empty chalices of Him that they be broken against the day. Even so, all things proceed unto the heavens and no broken thing abideth it. And he who falleth short and leaveth the chalices that they break, behold, the breaking is within him, and the mending is his. Yea, and there is no light within the heavens save the Father's face, and woe unto thee at thy mending, for He shall not look upon thee."

° The word "office" is used here in the religious ceremonial sense

And they were frightened, for within the multitude were them that feared the words would reach the priests and the high officials.

And Jesus perceived this and spake: "Fear not Truth, for she sootheth and healeth the wound she causeth."

And they said: There are more that hunger."

And He held high His hand o'er the bended head of him that had come unto Him, and spake: "Nay; this one is not filled. He hath asked 'How may a man know the Father?' and I answered thee, know His works; for therein is He. No fashioning of man holdeth the breath of Him, save that he who builded it took out of Him. Ye may know the false from the true by this thing. No thing liveth without it is of Him."

And they harked unto these things and stood long looking upon Him. And He spake not, but delivered the one who sought that he know the Sire unto his brothers. And they pressed upon Him, crying out: "Thou hast spoken that to know the great God, man must know His works. Whereon shall he look that he know them? Are the smokes of sacrifices His labor? The fasting and feasting, are these His works? What manner of labor doth He do?

And Jesus answered them: "Thou hast looked upon the works of Him since thine eyes oped. Thou hast heard from the lips of the priests the words of the prophets, wherein it is written He hath builded up the earth. Look then upon all things, mean or yet little, great or yet mighty, and this is His. The sun writes Him upon the skies, yet the shadows of the leaves tell more of Him, for they are beneath thine eyes."

Jesus Offers the Other Cheek

And they spake among them: "Look! Yon standeth the mad one and the fool! Bring him up, for his wisdoms have mighty walls, even though he holdeth no thing within them."

And it was true that they went up unto the lame one, who was Hatte, and spake: "Take thy woes unto Jesus Christus, for He is ministering unto the multitudes."

And Hatte said: "Thinkest thou He might fill the empty cup from which the wine hath spilled? Hast thou seen Hatte? He is gone!" And he called: "Hatte! Hatte! Come forth! Bring thy bowl and this man may fill it!" And he turned his anguished face unto them and spake: "See ye! He will not answer nor come forth. Call him, brothers, call him!"

And he drew him up proud and said: "Nay! Nay! Hatte is but an humbling, and I am the son of Tiberius – Tiberius, who hath her.[1] Knowest thou her? She is the young morn floating unto the day upon the night's breeze, and her feet twinkle as the stars. Her robe is the white morning's clouds tinted of the sun. Tiberius hath eaten her. Hatte seeth her bones gleam."

And he cried out aloud. And Jesus harked and spake: "What is this thing?"

And they spake in answering: "This man is beset of a devil. An evil spirit abideth him."

And Jesus smiled and said: "Nay; his words are bottomless. They hold not."

And He sought the spot where Hatte looked unto the skies, and his face was lighted up, and he smiled and cried out: "Theia! Theia! Behold thy son! Look upon the multitude! They have come unto him for to bow down and call him noble!"

And Jesus touched him, and he drew him away, crying out: "Nay! Nay! Thy touch is like unto hers!" And he shrunk even unto the hiding of his face.

And Jesus spake: "Art thou hungered? See! There is bread."

---

[1] Theia, his mother

And Hatte's face flamed, and he turned unto Jesus, and his great eyes burned, and he bit upon his lips and beat his hands one upon the other, and he spake: "Thou asketh is Hatte hungered? Ah, is Hatte hungered? List! He hath ne'er eat. Where is the bread? These eyes see it not."

And Jesus spake: "Give unto me thy heart that I may feed upon it, and I shall give thee mine."

And Hatte drew him high and smote the cheek.

And behold, a beauteous light brightened the loved countenance, and He turned unto him the other.

And they that had seen this thing cried out: "What! Thou dost offer the other cheek that he smite thee?"

And Jesus answered: "Yea, for a withered hand[2] may not know that that it doeth."

And Hatte hissed: "Give thou me the bread! It is not thine, but *my* sire's."

And the multitude cried out: "Nay, cast him down! He hath defiled thee."

And Jesus answered: "Nay; inasmuch as he hungereth, it is his freely. That which a man giveth, he should give forth freely, nor look for the returning."

And Hatte cried out curses and gnashed his teeth and frenzied unto the shewing of his madness. And when he was spent, behold, he fell down before Jesus crying out: "The earth is shut unto me! My brothers know me not. All men cloak within hate before me. Look! Even the multitudes draw them from me and would stone me." And he looked him troubled unto Jesus and spake: "As thou art a man, if thy words be true, why hath the Father that begat me and thee done this thing?"

And behold, Jesus raised His eyes, and His lips were hung of sweetness, and He touched Hatte's flesh. And Hatte cried: "Nay! Nay! Touch not this flesh! The touch seareth – 'tis hers!"

---

[2] Hatte had a lame hand and leg

And Jesus spake: "Hark!" and He pointed unto the westway wherefrom came forth clouds that told of rains. And behold the lightnings played the clouds. And Jesus said: "Look! Yon is the storm. It shall pass o'er the valley's places and the fields, and rains shall sweep and winds rage. Yea, and lightnings flash. Even then the sun shall follow.

"Love is the sun, and the wrath of men the lightnings; the sighs of men the winds; the tears of men the waters of the rains. And the sun of love followeth them."

And they spake: "What sayest thou?"

And Jesus answered: "Behold, then when the fields stand clothed of the raiment of lilies and many blooms, what thing hath done it? – the sun, or yet the storm? That thou mayest know light thou shouldst know darkness."

And Hatte spake: "Yea, but how may he who ever troddeth darkness know light?"

And Jesus answered: "Each day that cometh lifteth the darksomeness. Like unto the scales of fishes the days shall fall. Man may not eat the flesh of the day, save that he live the hours, and no man eateth a fish who taketh not off the scales; even so, a man may not know his day until he hath taken off his scales of hours."

And Hatte looked unto Him and spake: "Thy words fill this head up and it falleth unto agonies. Behold, I hark, and within me crieth out: 'The Father hath done this thing, and thy brother loveth the Father, thereby would He make shadows o'er the Father's offending.' Thou didst lie unto me. Thou didst speak the Father abided within the temple.[3] Thou didst speak that thou wouldst tell unto Him of Thea and her flesh. Yea, and I sought the temple and was mocked."

And Hatte swayed and his eyes misted and he spake him: "What is this thing?" And he cried out: "The slaying! The

---

[3] Hatte was recalling what Jesus had said when they met as youths

slaying!" and ran from the midst of the multitude that laughed in mocking upon his madness.

And Jesus Christus spake in words that cut the airs: "He who calleth his brother a fool is in danger of the Father's wrath, for the fool is His son! Rebuke not, for rebuking hath a ne'er dying echo, and shall come back unto thee!"

And the multitude marveled and cried out words one unto the other, saying: "What manner of man is this who speaketh gentleness unto him that smiteth and crieth out against Him?" And they turned unto Him, and one among them spake: "What! Thou hast left this man that he flee?"

And Jesus lifted up His head, and His eyes sorrowed, and He said: "No man shall eat save that he look upon the bread; and how may a man, blinded of hate, see the bread?"

And they spake: "Thou didst minister unto him. Thou hast spoken wisdom, yet his ears take in not that that thou hast spoken."

And lo, Jesus said: "Thou hast seen not this thing. Behold, he is gone, yet the bread is living and shall be fit that he eat, even though he tarry."

And behold, afar there sounded the voices of many who railed against the one. And lo, a voice cut clear o'er all the dinning. And the multitudes looked and they spake: "The one hath sought yon, and crieth out unto his fellowman. Come, that we hark!"

And the loved of Him said: "Nay, we would list." And they stopped their words. And lo, the voice of the one came unto them, and, amid pealing laughter, the words: "Ha, ha, ha! He hath offered bread unto one who hath no bottom to his belly. This is folly. His bread is for men who labor not with hate as their fellow. No words He hath spoken mendeth e'en one wound. Yet they bow down unto Him and cry Him 'Master,' 'Lord.' Ha, ha, ha! They lift up a fool and call Him noble!"

And they that harked, when the words had ceased, spake unto Jesus, saying: "Didst thou take in this thing?"

And He raised up His hand and pointed afar unto the way of the storm's coming, and answered: "Man's day is even as the day of earth, and cloud shall come unto one even as unto another. And this have I spoken; that, even as thy brother in the flesh, shall the Son of Man know man's day, and even so the days of earth; that He shew unto them that He ministereth unto *thy* day, unto *thy* hunger, unto *thy* woe, in full knowledge of thy need."

And they spake: "Thou didst say that no broken thing abideth the heavens. How is this thing? Behold, yon man is filled of devils."

And Jesus answered: "The words upon thy tongue empty him not nor fill him. No thing that is broken abideth the heaven, for look ye, the heavens are not yet builded. He who is empty *shall* be filled. He that is broken *shall* be mended and brought together. It is written! For no thing He hath fashioned is broken save man. And this thing is true so that he who is set upon earth by the Father is set upon the building of heaven.

"In the Father's house are many mansions. Yea, and the Son of Man goeth before thee. Yea, proceedeth unto the Father that He prepare a place for thee. Look ye unto it. This is the labor of the mending, yea, the filling, yea, the building.

"Behold, the man that tarrieth, tarrieth heaven. He who breaketh a brother hath set the break unto heaven. This thing is true. And not until the building is taken up and set finished, and all men look upon their days as the building, shall the heaven be builded.

"Behold, men shall rise up and fall, thereby falling heaven. Men shall take up the broken and mend it, thereby mend the heavens."

And they spake: "Master, thy words confound us."

And He answered them: "Nay, not thee, but the earth's days that shall come, yea, and come. Yea."

A Man Should Love Them That Hate Him

And they marveled at the words He had spoken, and they said unto Him: "Tell unto us – tell unto us the filling of our hunger."

And He spake: "A man's tongue should speak not unto the seas of his brother's, but seek the small pools."

And they said: "Wilt thou then minister unto another?"

And He answered: "Bring him forth."

And they brought forth a one who cast him down and spake: "Master, I have given of my goods unto my brothers that they prosper, and no thing returneth unto me. Behold me! I am a man who loveth his flesh[∞] and hateth his enemy."

And Jesus took him unto Him and spake: "He who giveth should not look for the shadow of his giving to come unto him in return, for there shall be no sun of thanksgiving. And he who loveth them that love him, what thanks hath he? for there be sinners who do this thing. Yea, and he who hateth his enemies, what thank hath he? For there be sinners among all men who do likewise. But a man should love them that love him, thereby building up love. Yea, a man should love them that hate him, even so that the persecutions offered unto him shall exalt him; for therein is the rod by which man is measured."

And they spake, answering His words: "But no man doeth this thing. A man is a fool who would love his enemy, for did he clothe him within his love, then should he know not only the blade's point of him but its broad part."

And Jesus smiled and answered: "Nay, this is not the manner of loving. Love him as thy teacher; for he sheweth thee thy measure."

And they cried: "This thing is whole, and holdeth!"

[∞] His kin

Jesus Heals The Servant

12. And at a later tide, behold, within a certain city came Jesus Christus. And the fame of Him had swept like unto eating flames. All men knew His works. His words were like unto cooling cups unto the thirsted, and no man knew upon what road's-way he might come upon a cup.

And it was true that a certain man of office sent forth when he heard of His coming, saying: "Go unto this man who doeth wonders and bid that He come unto me. I am o'er my brothers; for within my household are them that go when my lips speak 'go' and come when my lips speak 'come.' The walls of mine abode are hung of rugs and my bread is of the whited grain's meal, yet am I unworthy that this man come unto me; for He hath that that causeth the riches of a man to turn unto dusts. Speak unto Him and tell that my well-loved servant hath lain him down and is smitten, and cause that He come."

And they spake: "But how is this that thou knowest He will heal thy servant?"

And the one made answer: "He hath but to speak the words and it shall be done."

And they sought Jesus and told unto Him of this thing, and behold, He answered them, saying: "Upon the footcloth of his faith shall I enter his household. The bread of faith shall lift up his servant and the wine of love shall succor him."

And He followed them that sought, and behold, when they had come unto the household of the man of office, he sent forth a servant who bore words that his master spake that He should tarry, for his master was unworthy that He come unto him.

And Jesus answered: "Return and say unto him, I am already within him; for in loving I have ministered and he hath eaten the seed and grown his faith."

And they entered the place and the man cast him down before Jesus.

And Jesus spake unto him: "Arise and shew me thy servant."

And the man pointed unto the inner place where, on the rugs, lay his servant. And he called: "Arminius![1] The Nazarene hath come."

And behold, the head of Arminius raised up, and his eyes were misted o'er of the falling away of the spirit, and he shook but made that he arise and murmured: "Jesus Christus, the Nazarene, whom she[2] seeketh!"

And it was true that Jesus called that they bring forth water and with His own hands bathed the fevered brow. And His words flowed sweet as a mother's sound unto her babe.

And the fevered lips of Arminius spake: "But to lose the blade of Rome! The yoke of the oxen to fall upon a noble's back!"

And it was true that Jesus heard all that had been, and He spake words of comforting, and within the words of comforting shewed the light of promise. And He sat Him long, and His hands busied, and they who had brought Him forth watched, and behold, the head of Arminius sank upon His bosom, and he slept even as a babe tired of the day's hours.

And his sleep-heavy lips murmured: "Arminius, thou hast lost office but to find a Brother." And he smiled amid his dreaming.

And they that saw spake: "He shall awake refreshed, yea, renewed."

And they called the name of Jesus blessed. And the man of office spake words of thanks unto Him.

And He said: "This is not done save through thy faith; for upon the footcloth of thy faith have I come unto thy household."

---

[1] A Roman noble who gave up his position to help Mary, daughter of Flavius, find Jesus
[2] Mary, daughter of Flavius

And He departed upon His way, and taught the people within the city.

Mary, Daughter of Flavius, Anoints the Feet of Jesus
13. And when the hour had grown late, a man sought Him out who was a Pharisee, and spake unto Him bidding Him come unto his board and eat of meat and break bread.

And the multitude said: "Look! He goeth then unto the house-hold of a Pharisee! Is this thing right or meet?"

And He answered: "Behold, the bread I offer shall be eaten within any man's household who shall receive it. Even so there unto his board do I sit and break it."

And they shook their beards, but He followed and with Him His loved. And some among them that came unto the eating of bread questioned: "How is this that thou feastest and the disciples of John fasted much nor supped?"

And Jesus Christus spake, and His lips smiled: "Thou dost rebuke John and his disciples that they fasted much and supped not. Yet thou speakest within thee, 'Here is he who cometh and glutteth upon flesh and bread, and suppeth much.' And I answer thee saying: 'That that proceedeth from out John fed not upon bread nor sup, yet liveth; even so that that proceedeth from out my lips hath not succor from bread nor wine.'"

And He broke a loaf and dipped it within the wine and eat therefrom; even did He take of the meat and offer unto them that sat with Him. And as they ate, behold, there came forth a woman whose head was binded up of cloth, and she bore an alabaster box. And her hand smote the door's-way and she spake words unto them within that they leave her look upon Jesus.

And they turned and spake: "Depart, woman! We see thee not."

And behold, she swept swift up unto the feet of Jesus and oped the box, and the scents of the ointment crept the airs. And she touched the bruised feet of Him with her hands and wept o'er the bruises, and her tears flowed unto the dropping upon His flesh. And she unbinded her head and left her locks fall and wiped them, and took up the ointment and soothed the bruises. And her eyes she lifted not, but her lips murmured: "Thy words are like unto the stars that light the night, yet thy feet are bruised of stone."

And they that saw this spake: "This man is no prophet, for He would know what manner of woman was this." And they said: "This is a wanton, a she-one, not fit that she touch the flesh of one called clean. She is a Magdalene called Mary, the woman of the servant Arminius."

And behold, Mary fell upon her face and hid within her locks, and her lips moved and the words spake: "Nay, nay, it is not true. I am free of Rome, and this," and she touched the alabaster box, "is the last of Rome's goods; the ointment of folly shall soothe the wounds of Him, thereby buying fullness for emptiness."

And they that looked upon this spake unto Him saying: "Behold, this woman is unfit that she touch thy hem. Look upon her! She is a wanton and hath come unto the house of the righteous."

And Mary arose not, but let her face to hide within her locks. And lo, Jesus arose and spake unto them who harked, saying: "What man among ye hath come that he bear balm? Behold, her hands have come filled of ointment. Her locks hath she let down that she dry her tears that fell upon the bruising. What man among ye hath done this thing? A man's words may build paths, but behold, doth he set upon a way unto his labor, then his legs should trod the path. Even so a man speaketh righteously, yet his hands lie them idle. Let him that hath called her wanton shew his ointment. Let him that hath spoken her a magdalene call her name blessed, for behold, her hands have o'ercome her sinning."

And they marveled at His words and cried out against the woman, and spake that such a one should hide her face. And behold, Jesus said: "Woman, arise and shew thy face!"

And Mary arose and parted her locks, even so that her pure face shewed. And the cheeks gleamed of drops, and her full lips trembled, and her bosom heaved, and she looked unto them that stood within the place. And Jesus spake unto them, saying: "Behold, a man's sin is like unto a door. It turneth upon a thong and the thong is the thing that causeth it to ope and to shut. Thereby the thong is the door. What man herein knoweth the thong that hath oped the door unto this woman, or yet shut it?"

And Mary fell down unto the stoned floor before him, crying out: "It hath come, the sun! It hath come to light the dark!"

And Jesus spake unto her, saying: "Arise! Thy faith hath forgiven thee. Thy sin is overcome."

And they looked upon her, and some among them backed their thumbs and shrugged, and others oped eyes that saw new light. And Jesus spake: "Depart, and peace be unto thee."

And Mary lay the alabaster box upon the floor and oped its pit, and behold, tears fell within it, and she put unto it its cover and gave it unto the hands of Jesus. And He held it up before them that looked and spake: "Her casket of jewels also hath her hands delivered. Behold, the herbs of Heaven shall be refreshed with these."

And they departed, and the morn found them that had harked, filled of wonder and fear; for no man might speak the forgiving of sin save that he make his sacrifices at the holy spots. And they were fearful among them.

A Woman Who Touches Jesus Is Healed
14. And it was true that afar and near the fame of Jesus Christus spread forth, and it shewed within the byways and highways that He need not trod that He be known. And

where'er He sought unto, behold, His fame went before, even as the lightenings foretell the storm. And at a later tide, word went forth that He would seek out Jerusalem even though them that loved Him feared His going thereto. For the word of the mighty one[*] had gone forth since the fame of Jesus had spread, that he feared His might, and that he believed Him the risen John. Even did the words speak that He was a prophet of old and arisen. And it filled them that followed the teachings of Jesus full of fear, and they spake unto Him, saying: "It is well that thou shouldst not seek Jerusalem, inasmuch as thy fellowman speak o'er that they should of thee." For Jesus had chided them that they spread not His words, save unto them that hungered, and not unto them whose ears deeped for the filling. And He had looked upon them not but gazed afar and answered them: "Why fear? For it is written upon the sky that the Son of Man shall be delivered unto the people. Yea, that He shall arise and shew His flesh even before their eyes, for no man may destroy Him."

And they took not in that that He spake unto them, and answered Him, saying: "Look thou, Master, the multitudes press upon us. See! They come like unto the waves of water unto the shore, even to be stopped by thy smile, even as the tides follow the sun's and moon's going."

And behold, they pressed upon Him and they that loved Him clung close unto His side and made that they send them away from the side of Him, crying out: "How may we proceed when thou dost press upon us?"

And it was true that Jesus spake: "Who hath touched me?"

And they answered: "Behold, how may we tell unto thee who hath touched thee? Even as a tree that swayeth within the winds, thy body doth sway with the press."

---

[*] Herod, the tetrarch

And He spake once more: "Who hath touched me?" And His eyes fell upon a woman who knelt at His feet, crying out: "Behold me, Lord! I am before thee."

And He said: "I have answered thee. Inasmuch as thou hast touched me and thy touch fell in faith, it is done. Arise! Thou shalt be whole, for behold, the new light sheweth no shadows."

Jesus Feeds the Multitudes

And the loved of Him spake: "Lord, they have followed and are wearied upon the way. How then mayest thou speak unto them or yet minister when their bodies hunger and their bellies cry out for meat and breads?"

And He answered: "And thou art then chosen that thou shalt build up faith!"

And they said: "Then wouldst thou that we go forth and buy of meats and breads for all of these?"

And He answered: "Nay. Leave me that I speak with them."

And behold, He sent up His silvered voice, saying: "Depart ye and set down that we feast." And He spake unto them that He loved: "Go thou and set them down within tribes, fifty unto the tribe."

And there were many, and behold, the loved cried out: "Master, this is folly, for behold, there is naught save two fishes and a loaf."

And Jesus smiled and spake: "Do thou as I have spoken."

And they did the thing, and behold, they sought out a stone that stood high, and Jesus went Him up unto its summit and sat, and they came unto Him, saying: "Master, it is done. Thou didst speak that we set them down and it is done. Yet here are the fish and the loaf."

And Jesus took out of their hands the fish and the bread, and holding it up high, spake words of supplication unto the Father. And behold, them that looked upon Him harked. And He broke the fish, even so the bread, unto many bits. And lo, He sat and His voice lifted up, and He taught them in parables, speaking of days as ships, of men as grains, of earth as fields, of love as water, and of the Father's love as bread. And they harked, and were full of the spirit. Even did their eyes fill up of brightness and their faces shew the bathing of the spirit, and no man among them hungered. Even did they cry out: "I am full. Yea, Lord, why hunger? We are feasted."

And He spake on, and the twelve that He loved were as baskets that plucked up the broken crumbs that they hold them for the feeding of yet more of hungered. And it wore unto the coming of the eve and still they sat. And some among them pressed upon Him and spake: "Master, it is told that thou hast been found shining like unto some white light even as thou didst pray. Yea, eyes that have looked upon thee have lended their seeing unto lips that have told it."

And He answered: "No thing is wondrous. Behold, the words that build, of earth's waters, wines, may make light of darkness. No thing may hunger that is filled of the spirit of the Father; for the body crieth out only when the spirit is barren. For upon earth standeth men whose bodies are fatted and their spirits wasted racks."

And they listed unto His words, and when they had taken them in, behold, they knew not of what He had spoken.

Jesus Teaches About the Birth of the Holy Ghost

And it was true that one among them drew nigh and spake: "Master, what is the Father's labor that He set such as yon multitude upon earth, for there be not one man within ten that the earth hath need of."

And He answered the one, saying: "Behold, the Father manifesteth Himself in them all, and within their atoms is builded up great things. From out their blood cometh new men of office. Out of their bone is the bone of earth renewed. Yea, and their love is a mighty thing that may build from out itself a mighter work. For all of these hold them lowly, thereby, e'en though they know not their God, they deny Him not. Even so He dwelleth within them and they welcome Him.

"The Father is like unto an everlasting stream. He poureth Him about the universe. Yea, He is that upon which the universe hangeth. Behold yon multitude! They know not this thing, yet there be men among them whose hands up and down in labor for the Father, their eyes blinded and their ears not oped, yet He is within them, and thou mayest see Him within their eyes.

"He who denieth me denieth not the Father, inasmuch as his flesh is weak and his eyes oped but unto that his forefathers hath seen. Yea, and doth his lips deny me and his heart love my flesh, even so hath he acclaimed the Father.

"Man's words are but the scales upon the flesh of him, like unto the scales of fishes. Yea, and men of earth should cast the scales unto waste and eat the flesh. Doth a man of earth deny me, he denieth not the Father, inasmuch as I am not Him, but of Him, even as my brother.

"Go I unto him calling out that he acclaim me, and he denieth me, it is well, and he hath *not* denied the Father. Go I unto my brother once more crying out that he acclaim me, and he denieth me, but holdeth within him his counsel of his God, thereby again he hath not denied the Father. Go I unto him thrice crying out that he love me as his brother, but o'er me his God, and he denieth me the love, then hath he denied the Father. Go I unto him crying out that he love the Father and thereby share of his love with me, his brother, and he doeth this, behold, his spirit is cleansed and the Holy Ghost is born. Yea, like unto a white dove shall it descend unto thee, bearing the Sign, which is peace within thee.

"Thereby the Holy Ghost is not the Father and the Son within thee, but thee within the Father and the Son. Oh, ye sons of men! Think ye upon this and ponder it within thy hearts. Within thy hand is the taper that may light the Great Light. He, the Father, or yet the Son, may not proceed unto thee. Nay, but thou shalt proceed upon the path of love unto the Father and the Son. The High Throne waiteth thy coming, and even though the ages have preceded thee, still it standeth empty for thee! The Father's arms ope; wilt thou tarry?"

Jesus Continues His Teaching

"Look ye! *Man* is not complete. Behold, he is like unto a river that seeketh the sea and is beat and bruised waters that fret to find the sun. And the sun is even as the Father, for it taketh all the waters of earth back unto the source wherefrom it hath fallen. How know ye but that the waters of the earth be the tears of angels shed in sorrow, yet in mercy causing beauteous things to spring up?

"Man is not complete. Behold, how may he then take in all things? He is new, when the ages are old. Yea, and a new vat holdeth not well the wine. Then would the vine's man rebuke his vat? The sons of men have been set upon His lands and it is not the Father's will that he fail.

"Behold, I bring ye naught but the thing thou mayest balm all bruises with – *Love*. Nor do I cry out 'follow me,' but 'follow the way unto Him.' Oh, brothers! Do ye not receive me, remember, within thee keep the counsel of thy God! Cry out unto Him: "Father, hath my brother passed and I lifted not up mine eyes but saw thy light, forgive me, for I knew Him not. Hark, hark, oh, Father, hark!' Do this in contriteness and I promise ye the Son shall pass e'en so close that thou shalt see His smile.

"Oh, the blood of the tribe of David shall weep! Yea, and the tribes of Judea wail, for they shall be cast down. Among them shall I have trod, yea, ministered unto them in loving. Judea is full of loving within their hearts, but behold, the Son of Man shall be delivered unto the hands of glut. Yea, His blood shall make the tabernacle like unto an isle sunk afar. And ages shall cast stones at her[α], and sail new ships that bear new bread unto her people. Yet shall she stand! For she is not walls and stones, but the heart of the Jews! I say unto thee: Look unto what hath been. O'er the sea of blood shall the Son of Man walk, even upon its waters, unto the tabernacle, even within the holy spot. And the priests *shall* fall down and cry out: 'Christ!' Cease thy waiting, oh, Judea! Seek that thou dost make born the Holy Ghost!"

And they that harked marveled, and the words sunk within their hearts, but they feared, and some among them that listed would to know but might not know the fullness of the words. And no man arose that he depart.

And when the sun had sunk, lo, Jesus stood Him up and looked unto the way unto Jerusalem and spake: "Jerusalem, thou shalt stone me! Ye will not of the water and I would offer it, for a hand shall dash the cup."

And He withdrew, and His loved followed. And they spake unto the multitude: "Depart! It is finished. Peace be with thee!"

And the multitudes departed, and Jesus sought with His loved unto a new spot upon the way.

Master, Who Among Us Is the greatest?

15. And lo, the priests of the temples shook before the power of Him who unraimented them, who held God up unto the people, even lifted up the Holy Veil. They spake against this unto the tribes and called it the work of an heritic against the people. And still the tribe's men saw their God within the words of the Nazarene. The Jews and Rome's men were filled of the wonders He had done. Word had come that before Him multitudes bended low, that beneath His hands all sorrow vanished, the eyes of the

---

[α] Judea

weeping smiled; that no man who passed Him upon the road's-way might pass in knowing that he had met the God. For His words were like unto no man's. His wraths were anguish bathed of mercy, His sorrow was the tears of happiness, His wisdom like unto a breaking day, faint unto thee, and as tides swept, fairer, brighter; and when thou hadst wearied, behold, His wisdom was like unto the night's rest.

And it had come that multitudes had cried out: "Master, who among us is greatest?"

And He had taken unto His breast a babe and let His blessed lips to lay upon the golden crown and had spoken: "Behold the undoer of Heaven! I say unto ye, no man whose faith is not like unto one of these may know the Father. The fields of earth are like unto man, o'erfull of grain. Then how may ye become greater who are already full? Behold ye, he who filleth up on mighty things may forget bread! But the babe thirsteth for its mother's breast and knoweth not why nor yet whither from the fount. Except as thou becomest as one of these, thou mayest not see the Father. Behold ye the eyes of this one! Unto all earth it turneth fearful, yet unto its mother, knowing. Even so the son of man shall be.

"Oh, the folly of man! He plucketh up the sea's drift and storeth it, when, behold, the waters sing the song of knowing. Fill ye not up of wisdom, but of righteousness and mercy, for this is the bread of wisdom. The sea of wisdom rocketh upon a foundation of faith. Yet men there be who would know the foundation, and they shall drown! All that be of the Father be, like unto Him, of all, in all, yet not therein for the laying on of hands. Should then the Father be delivered unto man that he might lay hands upon Him, behold, he would set him down and play with Him like unto stones that might be cast. Yea, and at some morrow, behold, like unto a babe who hath no wisdom, would he cast Him!

"The river must seek a sea, the brook the river, the mountain the sky, and man his God. Else there is no going upon the way, but the end of all things. The Father is the mighty river that circleth the universe. Seek Him! Seek Him! Seek Him! And be empty for the thirst for Him! Earth's wisdoms are but the smiting that causeth thee to be greater cups for the filling. Care ye not for the wisdom that smiteth thee. Leave it for to smite, and remain thee but the cup. Forget not that thy hand shall bear the cup unto the River."

All of this had come and Jerusalem knew the fullness of such wisdom. And lo, it was true that word came that Jesus Christus was upon His way thereto, and much wonder spread among the people. Even though His feet had known the streets of Jerusalem, Jerusalem knew Him not, for the wick of His wisdom was then not yet lighted.

Jesus Enters Jerusalem

16. And the morrows sped unto a certain morn when the out-ways shewed the multitudes pressing upon Jesus, and His loved following Him. And behold, He rode upon an ass, and within His hand was the branch of a fig, the sign of fruiting. And they followed Him, crying out: "Messiah! Lord! King of kings!" Even did they unloose their headbands and their mantles and cast them down before Him that His ass walk o'er their cloth. And the gate's man, even of Rome, cast the gate ope that He go therein unto Jerusalem's heart, even though He should find not rest.

And it was true that when they had come within, the multitudes of the city's people came unto Him, and He sat upon the ass and spake unto them of Jerusalem and the Jews, for His blood lay close unto Him, yea, sorrowed Him.

And they spake unto Him, saying: "Master, Rome is within the land of the Jews. Yea, even Jerusalem hath she filled up of Rome."

And He answered them, saying: "Weep thou, oh, brothers, weep! Leave thy tears to flow for the tribes to come, for Rome shall slay their sheep of sacrifice, and betray them."

And they cried out: "Ope up thy mouth and leave forth words unto the Father that He make fire to descend upon them."

And Jesus answered them: "I am not come to destroy man but to deliver him from the serpent that crusheth. I am not come to unbuild, but to build up. No man shall call unto the Father that He send destructions. Nay; man shall not look unto Him for aid in such prayer. He who shall unbuild evils, doth build. Ye may not undo by undoing, save that the unbuilding be done in truth and not evil intent.

"Oh, ye of Jerusalem, hark! What is the law? Thou shalt not kill! Would ye then blade ye? For blade hungereth that it clatter upon its brother. The undoing that shall build shall be born of bloods.* This thing shall be. Even the Son of Man shall write the law, Thou shalt not kill, in His own blood. Yea, and this is the first seed for a greater harvest. Even so shall there be hosts that shall write upon the earth's sides, 'Thou shalt not kill,' in their bloods. Aye, and from out the flood of birth-blood shall come forth the thing that shall unbuild and thereby build!"

And they harked, but took not in the fullness of this, and cried out: "Nay, Master, who would destroy thee or yet slay thee?"

And He smiled Him sorry upon them and spake: "The sun that hangeth o'er Jerusalem shall look upon the thing I have spoken."

---

*By the shedding of blood

Jesus Drives Out the Martsmen

And they asked Him: "Goest thou unto the temple?"

And He answered: "Yea, after the manner of my tribe, for I am what I am, a Jew."

And it was true that they were filled of what was within Him, for His eyes shone, and His lips smiled soft and wistful, and His words fell sorried, even as though they came from out a throat that knew tearful eyes. And it was true that the coming together of the people brought forth ones of Rome who listed, and the bladesmen gathered them that they watch what would come to pass. And them within the market's bins came forth and joined unto them that followed Him, the Nazarene, and He went His way upon the ass unto the temple.

And behold, it was high noon, and the pool shewed bright, and the temple's doves wheeled within the sky and circled back unto the temple as the people came unto the spot. And lo, upon the steps unto the temple's doors squatted beggars. And men lay upon their sides upon the stones, and before them lay their wares. And the day was filled of their crying out. Even amid the chants of the priests within the temple place came floating, to echo against the alters, the crying out of wares. Even did the waresmen seek within the very threshold, barting with them that came without. And the priests looked not upon this, for unto the priests' hands they that barted delivered a sharing of what fell unto them, and thereby the priests took out of the people of their gains. And Rome knew this thing, and took of the priests a sharing of the sharing.

And it was the time when the martsmen cried loud that Jesus Christus came unto the temple and came Him off the ass and walked among them that beset the steps unto the temple's place. And when He had come unto the topmost stone of the temple's way, behold He turned. And the Rome's men stood at the base looking upon Him, for it was feared that the Jews, beneath the sound of His voice, would break forth. And when the eyes of Jesus fell upon the men of Rome He drew Him up unto His utmost, and wraths mounted His eyes even so that they looked heavy and fulled of sorrow, and His hands shook as He held them forth and spake and pointed unto the Rome's men, saying: "It is written that the Father's house should be the house of prayer, and prayer is the puring waters of the soul, and thou hast made it a den of thieves! Thinkest thou that the blade of office shall set fear within me? Nay! Hark ye!" And His voice rang clear and He took up a lash of knotted thongs and let it free upon the air and brought it down upon the back of a Jew who offered wares, crying out: "Be gone! Cast thee down within the dusts, for thou hast offended the God!"

And He swept unto another and let fall the lash, crying out: "Who art thou who may bring forth bart unto Him who barteth not?"

And He swept him on, and His cheeks flamed, and He cut upon the flesh of one who begged, and spake: "Go thou! For thou art come begging unto Him who giveth freely!"

And He passed Him on unto one who offered many colored stuffs, crying out: "Get thee gone! For who art thou who offereth vainglorious stuffs before His face who knoweth no thing that is vainglorious! Oh, my brothers! Where art thou, that thou wilt leave ones to deliver unto thy hands stuffs to set before the face of God?"

The Rich Man and Poor Woman

And it was true that as He smote the mart's ones upon the stoned way, there came forth a one whose robes shewed him of high office among the Jews, and he stepped him down unto the spot and looked at what was. And the eyes of Jesus saw this thing. And lo, there came forth a woman from out the temple's place. And she was of the hosts,° nor was she clothed in raiment that told her a man's woman, but within the sign of mourning. And the eyes of Jesus looked upon this thing, and He cried aloud unto them that listed as He brought down the lash upon the back of the man of office: "Look ye! It is far o'er an easier task that a camel may pass through the eye of the Needle than that a rich man may enter the Kingdom of Heaven."

And the Jews harked, for they knew of the gate which was called of this name, and the camel men came them and the camels kneeled that they passed through.

And Jesus cried aloud: "Look ye! A camel is for the pack, and no man who hath o'er his world's goods may stand him unpacked of follies. Behold her yon!" – and he pointed unto the sorrowed woman, - "she hath brought forth a coin which is mightier unto the sight of the Father than the camel's pack."

And the man of office looked upon Him and even though he was sorely tried, he cried not out but stopped that he list, being full of what was within Jesus that would come forth.

Jesus Prophesies Concerning Jerusalem and Rome

And the loved of Him cried out: "Hosannah!" "Lord!" "King!"

And the Rome's men spake unto them in a loud voice, saying: "Cease! Cease ye!"

And the Jews spake unto Jesus, saying: "Speak unto them. Say that they should not cry out aloud, for it is fearful unto us."

And the voice of Jesus arose, crying out aloud: "It may not be! For dost thou, oh Rome, cease their tongues, the stones shall cry aloud. The bone is builded by the Father and man shall make new flesh for the bone, but the tides

---

° A woman of the people, unmarried, and clothed in the garb of mourning

shall sweep, and the man-wrought flesh shall drop unto dusts and the bone remain. Ye may not stop the crying out of the stones, oh Rome! This is the bone. Thou mayest strip their throats of tongues but their bone shall remain, and the ages shall build them up and unbuild them and build them up once more, for they may not destroy them. New prophets shall take their places and offer new bread, but these prophets are false. Many shall come that shall speak out they are the Christ, even so that they are given the prophet's tongue. And I say unto ye, haste ye not forth that ye greet them, but wait the renewing of the old prophets. The hand of Rome is not upon the arm of God!"

And the Rome's men laughed, and the Jews were fearful, for this was against Rome and Jerusalem already smarted 'neath the lash. And Jesus stood Him higher upon the base of a pillar, and within His hand hung the lash. And behold, He held it up unto the seeing of the Rome's men and cast it o'er the multitude until it fell at their feet, and He cried aloud: "See! The Son of Man cometh uncrowned unto Rome's hands; yea, unbladed unto Rome's war. Yet Rome's foundation shall shake, and not one stone of the temple be left upon its brother! The precious stuffs of the holy places shall be grounded unto dusts beneath the mighty stones that fall. Yea, hark ye, my brothers of Jerusalem! Rome may unbuild ye, but she may not build ye up."

And tears flowed His eyes, and He raised them up unto the sky, and His hands spread forth and He cried: "Oh, Jerusalem, how would I have succored thee! How would the Son of Man have lain upon thy bosom; but thine eyes are blinded by the dusts of higher office. Oh, Jerusalem, Jerusalem the golden city, walled by the hands of the tribes that have found the promised land, I see thy very stones drop drops! Yea, Jerusalem, Jerusalem, the God hath knocked and thou didst not slumber, but, fearful, let Him go! Yet say I unto ye, my brothers, the breasts of

Jerusalem shall spurt new milk and the Son of Man shall nurture by it. The Jew's tribes brought forth the flesh of the Father, the Son of Man. Yea, and they shall fall unto child-bed again! For within their hearts shall He be born anew."

And His voice shook in sorrow, and He spake on: "Yea, when the Son of Man hath trod the path of ages and seen His hosts vanquished, seen His brothers broken against the day, and they upon the earth who have called Him brother forget Him and eat them lone the Father's bread, casting their bodies one 'gainst the other that they take their sharing, and He standeth waiting that they see Him, the new birth shall shew them!"

And He called: "Hark! Hark! Hark! Hark! Oh, Jerusalem, look ye! I am calling not thee now, but ever! For I am what I am, a Jew!"

And it was true that He came down among the Jews, and they fell upon Him, their eyes lighted with a new light and they spake: "We are answering thee!"

And He smiled and said: "Oh, ye beloved, I may not list, for I know!"

Rome's Men Question the Authority of Jesus

And the Rome's men came through the people and sought Him out and spake: "Thy hand doeth no service. Thou art even as a beggar. Thy followers are fed out of the bounty of the people. What manner of authority hast thou?"

And He answered them: "Look ye unto the sun! Ask him this."

And they marveled at this, that a man of no office should speak so, and they spake unto Him: "Knowest thou that among the Jews there be them that hate thee?"

And Jesus smiled and answered: "Look ye unto yon well! Know ye that beneath its waters are stones?"

And they spake: "But thy hands do no labor."

And He answered them, saying: "What wouldst thou?"

And they pointed unto a roadway, past the market's-way, wherein an ox stood fast with his wheeled pack. And they spake: "Go and deliver the ox unto its master out of the mires."

And He went unto the spot, and the people followed Him. And behold, He laid His hand upon the ox and it came forth. And He drove it thence out of Jerusalem's walls unto its master's abode. And they followed not His going without.

The Priests Confront Jesus

17. And the sun sunk and the night came thrice. And Jerusalem became a babel; for out of the temple the holy things were taken. And word came from out the mighty place that he who had done this thing should fall.

And the priests had list unto the ministering of Jesus and had called upon Him that He make known His authority. And He had confounded them with His learning, and filled up the people with His teachings. And there fell among the priests the wish that they might undo Him, for they feared the free-giving of the God would leave the temple bare. And they spake among them: "This, then, shall we hold as His work. For His hands labor not and His followers even so. They go fourth and cast the God unto the fields and roadways, and deliver Him unclothed unto the hands of the people. This, then, shall we call His work."

And it was true that the golden candlesticks that burned upon the altar of sacrifice were gone. And they sought Jesus and spake: "Hast thou done this thing? The lights are gone out of the temple."

And Jesus answered them, saying: "Wherefore hast thou need of light?"

And they said: "The bowls of office are gone also."

And He answered: "Wherefore hast thou need of bowls? For ye may not measure God."

And they spake: "The ashes of sacrifice are strewn."

And He answered them, saying: "It is well, for ashes are a dead thing, and the God a living thing. Hark ye! No Jew hath done this thing, for the temple is walled with his heart. Yet, I say, even so his heart is the temple, and no thing of office needeth he."

And they ceased. And Rome heard of this. And it was true that the wrath of the Jews was high, and they sought him who had defiled the temple.

Jesus Speaks of Mighty Signs

18. And Jesus Christus had taught within the temples, and the people were swayed as tall grass before the wind at His words. And He had spoken unto them of mighty signs, and had told once more that it was written that the Son of Man should be delivered unto the hands of sinful men and delivered up thence unto the hands of office, and should be slain and come forth at the third day, whole. And they marveled at all of this and spake within their beards: "This is in truth the Messiah. Yea, the Son hath come. Hath not His hands done wonders and His lips spoken the confoundment of the priests? Is not all of this foretold within the words of the prophet? Is it not written within the psalms of David, His glorification?"

And it had been true that Jesus had spoken unto them at a certain day, saying: "Ye shall see mighty signs writ upon the skies, and nations shall fall upon nations. Yea, and the skies shall spit forth fires; even so shall sea monsters ride upon roaring waves, yea, and wallow in their blood. And ye shall know this is the sign that the Kingdom shall come. Yea, Jerusalem shall be beneath the heels of the Gentiles. The waters of the tribes shall be dried up and they shall be cast unto the four corners of the earth. By all of this ye shall know the Kingdom is not by ye at the morrow, but by ye now. Oh, hark ye, my brothers of the blood! – for I am what I am, a Jew – it shall be within this dark day that the tribes shall be scattered as I have spoken, and the earth shall hold them up before their faces that the stones of the universe shall slay them. And I say me, this shall not be for Jerusalem, nor for the Jews, but that the Kingdom shall come.

"Behold, at a morn they shall awake and the Kingdom shall shew oped unto them, and the Son of Man shall shew, verily, even so that they shall see Him within them."

And they spake unto Him, saying: "Who then among us shall be greatest in the Kingdom?"

And He answered: "It is written, yet shall I speak it."

The Last Supper

19. And it was true that it was the feast of the Passover. And He spake unto them: "I would that I break this bread with thee, for know ye, this shall be the last bread before the coming of the Kingdom."

And they said: "But, Master, there is no household open unto us."

And He answered: "Go ye forth! Did I not send thee unpursed unto the byways, unscripted and without goods, and do ye lack aught?"

And they said: "No thing, Sire."

And He said unto them: "Then go ye forth, and ye shall come upon a man who beareth water and ye shall speak unto him, saying: 'Where within thy household is the feasting hall? The Nazarene hath sent us forth that ye make ready.' And he shall ope unto ye and therein shall ye eat."

And the Jews spake: "See! He hath prophesied." And they followed the loved of Jesus upon the way. And behold, they *did* come upon a man who bore water and they spake unto him as they were bidden, and he oped his house. And some among them departed that they bring forth Jesus Christus, and as they went thereto, Jesus turned unto Peter and spake: "Peter, the Lord God hath chosen that He cast my loved even as grains within a sieve that He find the tare. I have prayed that thy faith hold."

And Peter said: "Oh, my beloved! I would follow thee upon thy way, even though it led unto death."

And Jesus spake, and His eyes looked troubled: "Nay, Peter; before the cock crows thrice thou shalt deny me thrice."

And Peter denied this be true, and the disciples believed it not, nor did they that harked.

And it was true that they went unto the abode of the houseman, and they brought forth bread and wine and sat that they eat. And behold, the doors were shut, for Jesus Christus spake: "This would I with ye."

And when they had sat, behold He took up a loaf and broke it and spake: "This is my body that ye may feed upon it, for a man *must* have *bread* that he *know* the day. Take ye this in sign of this, for I go from thee."

And they spake: "Master, what speakest thou? This bread is thy body?"

And He answered: "Yea, for the flesh is the chalice that shall hold the wine of wisdom. Look ye unto it. Have I not builded my flesh as thine and dealt ye wisdom freely? Even so this flesh fed upon bread. This is the sign of the commonness of the flesh."

And He broke it up and eat therefrom. And they looked upon Him, and He delivered unto their hands the breaking, saying: "Take; eat in the sign."

And He sat and meditated long, and His lips moved and He spake unto them, saying: "The tribes to come shall pluck forth from the bowels of earth stuffs for the destruction of the building of God. With their own hands shall they fashion them, with their own strength shall they hurl them, with their own hate shall they cast them, dyed of poisonous stuffs. And they shall cry out: 'This is the wisdom of God.' I speak me, man's building, man's hurling, man's hating, is not of God. Man alone may beget hate or nurture it, for within the Kingdom it hath no rooting spot. Yea, and the earth shall shriek out against God, and this shall be near the Kingdom's coming. These tribes shall build up a mighty thing that shall stalk the earth, hideous of wrath, and I say me, beneath its feet shall be mankind. And when they have finished the building of this they shall call it a name, and behold, its flesh shall fall unto dusts before their eyes. And this is their folly. And the bones shall remain, and this is the bone of the righteous upon which the follied builded. And the falling away of the flesh shall leave it empty for the filling up of the Kingdom.

"All of this I have spoken unto thee, and it shall be ash unto the earth when this shall come, but beneath the ash shall the flame of my tongue burst forth."

And[*] the shades fell from beneath the tapers' lights and swept the walls. And His loved harked nor spake; and the bread was within their hands, for they listed and ate not. And He looked upon them, and behold, the head of John bowed, and he lay it upon the blessed breast and wept. And Jesus raised His arms and took him unto His bosom.

And it was true that His loved sat waiting, each hanging upon His word, and o'er their faces played the light and shadow like unto the foreshadows of the coming ages.

And He spake: "The spirit moveth me to tell thee all. Thou hast asked who among ye should be greatest. I answer ye I yet should speak. Let he who is greatest become as him that serveth, and let he who is least among ye become as him who eateth the meat served at the hand of him who serveth. Look ye! Am I not He whom thou knowest, and bear I not the Father's bread with mine own

---

[*] Patience prefaced the sitting commencing with this paragraph with a little prayer, which follows: "Oh, my beloved, give tongue to me to sing thy sorrows like unto a gladsome song! For I see thy bloody sweat like rubies gleaming in their triumph. I see thy crown of thorns bejeweled of them, and their glory fades beside the radiance of thy smile. Leave me, oh my Beloved, thy smile!"

hands? Thereby am I among ye. Hark! this say I: One among ye shall, with the sign of loving, deliver me up. And he is with me now, his hands upon the table. For this am I deeply sorrowful, for woe is he who denieth his God, for he is empty and shall seek his filling. For he *shall* come unto the Kingdom full laden."

And He arose and spake: "What! thou hast not eaten? This is the sign. Earth shall tarry. Yet I have sung unto the empty hills, unto my brothers; I have trodden their paths; I have known the stones; I have known the hunger of the flesh, that ye shall know the God is a jealous God and denieth not His Son His brother's dealing. Ponder this within thy hearts.

"Let him who is without purse seek one; let him who hath no sword strip him and purchase one – yea, a purse of wisdom of the Father, and the sword of righteousness. I am filled of the bread for ages. Yea, this leaven I put within thee. Make ye it threefold fruitful. Look ye unto it! I shall give ye the tongue of confoundment. They shall persecute ye, and among ye are they that shall suffer death. Thy tears shall write scripts for new men. Thy blood shall buy the birth of newness within wisdom-old hearts, for the God, the Father, is ever new, and no wisdom of Him is ever old.

"Through the bond of flesh am I earth's. Nor shall I forsake her, neither my blood. When I shall look upon the blood of the tribes[∞] persecuted, behold, shall I stand beside them waiting. Yea, when the earth shall seem for to deny me and decry my Father, there beside her shall I wait. For earth hath an end, even so tribe, even so mankind; but the Kingdom hath not an end. Behold, the riven fields *shall* heal; the split mountains *shall* fall; the sea's water *shall* dry; mankind *shall* cease; yet shall I wait, for the eternities are ever waiting.

[∞] The Jews

"All things shall be completed therein, then renewed and completed. Thereby the complete awaiteth renewing and the renewed awaiteth the completing. Behold, the hour is upon us!"

And they harked, and He commanded them: "Eat, for ye shall remember me in bread!"

And they ate slow. And He took up a vessel of wine and poured forth a cup and spake: "Behold thou this! This is the covenant of blood – the sign of birth, not death; not many cups, but one, thereby shewing the Son of Man is one of ye."

And He held it high and spake: "Father, behold thy Son!" And He supped the cup, and with His wet lips kissed its brim for His brothers. And lo, the spot was bright of a new light that shone from Him like unto a radiance. It streamed His eyes like the beams of a star, and His hands seemed for to stream gentleness. And they that looked upon Him were filled, not of wine but of spirit.

And He breathed: "This is the Holy Ghost, the sign of peace within thee!"

And they fell silent before Him. And He stood long, wrapped, like unto an illumined chalice that poured living wine. And His loved knew within them the tide and the day had come, and saw the shadow that man cast upon Him.

And He was sorrowful. And they came unto Him, and He passed unto their hands the cup, saying: "Drink, in the sign!"

And they sat and waited His words, for He seemed that His flesh chafed and His spirit would flee.

And when they had waited long, behold, He arose and spake: "Unto thee do I deliver the watchword of the Kingdom – Mercy. Unto thee do I deliver the key – Faith. Unto thee do I deliver the Kingdom – Love."

And they arose and bowed before Him and He said: "Peace be with ye, yet I know it shall forsake ye."

And it was late hour, and afar the sounds of Jerusalem sounded through the dark. And He spake unto them, saying: "I would go up into some spot where I may hear the stillness."

And they said: "Unto the mount, Master? Unto the garden?"

And He answered: "Yea, for upon the mounts sound the heights of earth's sounds, and I would know the stillness that I hark unto the small voices."

Jesus in the Garden

20. And they departed unto the garden. And He withdrew from them, even though they would follow Him.

And they spake unto Him, saying: "Shall we make ready swords to defend thee and stand waiting, fearful of them that might seek?"

And He answered them: "Nay. The Kingdom of Love is complete; it is the fearfulness *and* the sword. Await!"

And He departed within the garden's place. And they harked long unto His voice, raised up like unto a song, wooing, tender, pleading, gladsome, fretting to away! And His form shewed touching the earth with His hands, pressing the green things unto Him, looking unto the skies, turning all ways. And once more His voice arose like a mighty wind speaking monstrous* things, filling the emptiness of all things till it seemed that the dead stones had taken Him in.

And He knelt Him down and looked up on high, and behold, no light was there. And His voice sounded amid the dark: "Father, behold thy sons!" And He spake more unto the heavens, saying: "If it be thy will, the bitter *shall* be sweet! If it be thy will, leave the bitterness unto me and by my supping sweet the cup. May it pass from me, sweet, unto thy sons!"

---

* In the sense of tremendous

And from the East shewed the new day's coming. And He arose and held His arms wide to greet her, and His lips spake: "Father!"

And He sought slow through the thick growth, pausing to pluck a branch and kiss it, plucking up a stone, to smile and leave it fall. And the dews of night glisten upon His raiment. And He sought His loved, bathed of the Holy Ghost.

And lo, He came upon them, and they had wearied and slept. And He stood within the young light and looked upon them and smiled, and spake: "Sleep, oh earth! Ye *shall* wake! The day knocketh thee. The stars have fallen out of the heavens and given place unto the sun of Love. Awake! Do ye tarry? Then sleep, for thy waking surely cometh. The Son of Man hath not a spot whereon to lay His head save the bosom of Heaven."

And it was true that there shewed men of Jerusalem who sought the spot, and Jesus looked upon their coming like unto one who awaited them he knew.

And He said: "Where hath Judas gone from among ye?"

And His loved answered: "He sought the temple that he make his praying. He hath gone unto the priests for to pray."

And behold He smiled and spake: "The tare. Within thee forgive him."

And it was true that as the men of Jerusalem came unto the spot they shewed to be men of office and some of the priests. And it came to pass that Judas came from out their midst and fell upon the shoulders of Jesus Christus and kissed Him. And Jesus turned and held His oped hands unto them that came and spake: "By the sign of love is love delivered up."

And they that sought called out against Him as a tongue that drove the people out of the temple. And it was true that the loved looked upon Judas and knew that the prophecy had come. And Judas looked not unto them but departed among them that sought.

And they spake unto Jesus, saying, for there were men of office that listed unto His words for heresy: "Art thou the Son of God?"

And He answered not, knowing their meaning. And they said: "Make thee a wonderwork, since thou canst do these things."

And He answered them not, but stood looking far; nor sought He out with His sorrowed eyes, Judas.

And they spake unto Him, saying: "Thou hast perverted the people and driven them forth out of the temple."

And the priests bore upon Him charging all of this. And He spake unto them answering: "Whyfore hast thou not lain thy hands upon me within the temple?"

And the priests took this in and spake unto Him, saying: "But thou hast o'ercome the words man should speak of the God, for do ye deliver the God unto the people that they may eat them as bread, lo, He shall become as a naught."

And Jesus answered them, saying: "Nay; doth the God be delivered unto the people, they shall fat and thou shalt lean."

And the Romans harked unto what the priests had spoken, and they urged them that they decry Him. And lo, they binded up His eyes and smote Him upon His flesh, crying out: "What thing hath smitten thee? Prophecy! thou canst then tell!"

And He answered not. And His love drew nigh that they defend Him, and, behold, the Rome's men lay lash upon them and drove them forth before them. And they made fast the hands of Jesus and sought the way unto Jerusalem's heart. And lo, as they passed upon the way through the street's ways the Jews looked upon Him and went unto their households and shut up their doors, even so that no Jew shewed.

The Trial of Jesus
21. All of this filled up the morn. And it was true that Jesus Christus had been taken forth unto the temple and thence unto Rome's hall. And the mighty one had known that the Jew, Jesus, was of Galilee, and behold, he had builded up within him a thing for to do that Rome fall not within the displeasure of the Jews. Then would he deliver Him up unto him who sat upon the seat of judgment for His land;* thereby Rome should be clean. And when they had brought forth Jesus Christus, behold, they told that He had spoken treasons against Caesar, and would do no homage before the name of Caesar, speaking out that His Father sat o'er the kingdoms of the earth, and no man might call his name Caesar and cause the son of such a Sire for to make homage. And the mighty one harked but spake not. And they made more words, saying that He was the Son of the God, and this was blasphemy. And they made much of this, speaking: "This is an offense worthy of death."

And the mighty one said: "Art thou the Son of God?"

And Jesus answered: "Thou hast spoken it. Should my lips have spoken it thou wouldst not believe."

And the mighty one spake: "What manner of words tellest thou the people that setteth them against thee?"

And Jesus answered him: "I am come to lift them up, and they exalt themselves from the earth unto the lifting up. Yea, from the prostration upon their faces they look for the coming of a new day."

And the mighty one made more of words, and in answering got no thing that might wax his wrath.

And he turned unto them that had brought Him and said: "I will not of this barting. Seek ye unto the spot where the

---

*Herod Antipas

judge of His land abideth. I have found no thing that might cause Rome to slay Him."

And they took their words unto the judge of the land of Galilee, and lo, as they sought therefrom, no Jew shewed upon the way save them that had been at the barting. And when they had come unto the spot, they cast the form of Jesus before them and pressed upon Him unto His bearing down, and tore at His raiment. E'en did they spat upon Him, for the Rome's men had seen His teachings and were filled with wild words that told that from the lowly would He be lifted up. And believing that He, or yet Hatte, was the flesh of Tiberius, lo, they thought them to shew their hate of Tiberius in the smite of anything him.

And lo, it was true that they drove Him up unto the foot of the mighty-seat whereon sat the judge of Galilee's land.[∝] And they brought Him unto His knees before the mighty-seat and cried: "Make ye homage!"

And He moved not. And they smote Him, and His flesh shrunk, yet moved He not. And they brought Him down even upon His face before the mighty one, crying out: "Make ye homage!"

And He arose before the mighty one and stood Him up, nor bowed He His head.

And they spake unto the mighty one, when they had fallen upon their faces before him: "This man hath offended the Jews, for He calleth Him the Son of God, and this waxeth wrath among them."

And it was true that the mighty one had been filled of the teachings of Jesus Christus, and had taken in the words that had spoken that He had begotten wonders before the eyes of men, that had set wondering among the sages of the land; and he was filled of the desire that he look upon the man Jesus that he fill up of Him, thereby to know was He the flesh of Tiberius, as it had been told within the beards

---

[∝] Herod Antipas

of men. And he took in that the man Jesus was a Jew, for upon Him was the sign of the blood.

And he spake unto Him, saying: "Is this thing true?"

And He answered: "Thou hast spoken it. Have I not taught within the temple's places, among the priests, and they reached not forth their hands nor laid them upon me?"

And the mighty one spake: "But thou hast answered not. Art thou the Son of God? For mine eyes look upon thee and my lips would speak out, 'A Jew.'"

And Jesus Christus stood before him, His hands locked one unto the other before Him, and His head high, and He spake: "Thou hast spoken it. I am a Jew."

And the mighty one said: "But thou hast not answered. Once more, art thou the Son of God?"

And Jesus Christus spake: "Is this the mighty one who asketh this thing? Sire, thou knowest do I answer thou wouldst not believe."

And the mighty one spake: "Whyfore among the Jews wouldst thou defile the temple?"

And Jesus answered: "Nor have I done this thing. Within the temple is no thing that is not wrought of man. How then doth defileing be?"

And the mighty one knew that this was fearful, for the Jew's priests harked, and even though Jesus Christus swayed their people upon His words, their tongues sat within the throats of the people.

And he spake: "What manner of man art thou, for knowest thou not that thy words are defilement?"

And Jesus answered: "Nay; my words are the light. E'en though my blood shut the temple, yea, seal it up, it is man-wrought and shall crumble and the light enter."

And they harked, and the priests cried out: "Seest thou, O mighty sire, He hath uttered the defilement! For He knoweth not a temple, but taketh His God among the unclean! Yea, nor doth He look Him unto the sacred rites of the Jews nor payeth He tribute unto the sect, but maketh Him free among all men!"

And it was true that the mighty one harked unto them, for he was filled of pride that the man of Rome should deliver up his right unto him. Yet he was filled of the Jews and knew that their eyes burned living fires, that their hearts were full of this man, Jesus Christus, that they but awaited His word to arise, and he would not that their wrath fall upon him. And it was true that when he had spoken long and brought forth no thing save that that might offend the Jews, he turned unto them that had sought and spake: "Return ye! Go ye unto the Sanhedrin."

And it was true that one of the priests said: "Yea, bring Him forth before the temple's judges. Make Him utter the defilement."

And they bore Him out among them and mocked Him. Even did the servants of the mighty one bring forth tattered raiment of beauteous color and they arrayed Him. And lo, like unto the white moon that had come unto some glaring noon looked He! And yet His flesh bore the mocking even as a noble might take homage. And they called Him names of ribaldry, and His lips smiled. And they wondered among them that He breaked not nor wrathed.

And among them they spake: "This is the flesh of Tiberius."

And the Rome's men said: "Yea, this is true. Look ye! He knoweth His sire will lift Him up."

And they spake unto Him: "Is it true that thy sire shall lift thee up?"

And He cried: "Upon earth's folly am I exalted."

And they bore Him unto the household of one of the priests. And behold, within the court was kindled a burning heap whereby stood the servants that they make lights for the lighting up of the household at the later tide. And they brought forth skins and left before the fires unto the tide that they shewed hard and dried. And these they stripped into narrow thongs for wicking; thereby the scent of the green skin was gone. And they brought Him forth unto this spot.

And it was true that His loved sought Him out, fearful. And a one, a servant, looked upon Peter, who came unto the court seeking, saying: "Yon is he who is of this man's tribe. He is one of Him."

And it came to pass that they drew up unto Peter and spake: "Is this man He whom thou knowest and art thou of Him?"

And Peter, knowing that woe was upon him, answered: "Nay, I know Him not."

And lo, he withdrew unto the outer spot from the court. And one of the men servants spake unto him, saying: "Thou art one of His teachers. Thou knowest this man, Jesus Christus?"

And Peter said: "I know Him not."

And he came back unto the spot whereon stood Jesus Christus within the hands of the Romans and the priests and them that would lead Him unto sacrifice, and he looked upon Him. And one of the priests spake: "Is this man Jesus Christus?"

And Peter answered: "I know not."

And the cock crew thrice, and behold, Peter's eyes started ope, and Jesus Christus lifted His sorrow-heavy eyes and spake: "And unto thee, Peter, did I deliver the stone of my foundation. Yea, unto thy hands did I commend the very foundation of the temple I am come to shew – Faith; unto thee have I delivered the kingdom – Love, and thou art faithless."

And Peter fell upon his face, weeping. And they looked upon what had been and spake: "This man doth know Him."

And Jesus Christus said unto them: "Nay, he knoweth me not. His eyes are sealed, yet his heart shall ope them, for he hath the key."

And they brought Peter up unto Him and spake: "What manner of man denieth one he loveth? This is one thou wouldst claim as thy loved."

And Jesus Christus answered: "What manner of man denieth one he knoweth? Flesh *is* flesh. Flesh is flesh, and may thereby err. He who denieth me not his love, denieth me not. His lips have uttered words like unto scales upon the meat of fish."

And they spake: "What wouldst thou of him – that he acknowledge thee?"

And Jesus spake: "Look unto him! He doeth this."

And He took Peter unto Him and kissed him upon the cheek. And they that had looked upon all of this marveled, for the man broke not, and they fell unto words among them.

And the Rome's man took out of the servant's hands the skins that were green and slitted them, thereby making of them thongs, in which they tied knots, knotted o'er stones. And they made of these lashes, crying out: "This is the Son of God! Behold ye, O ye Jews!"

And the Rome's men brought down the thongs upon Him and drove Him through the street's-ways and thence the byways that they might shew the Jews what had been. And behold, the households were shut. And as they shewed, the bin's men that had remained put up the bin's cloths and hid. And they brought Him up unto the temple, and the Rome's men spake: "What manner of judgment may thy priests speak upon Him, for they have not the power that they may slay?"

And they spake among them that they should seek out the Rome's court and make known that it was the wish of the people that the man be delivered up unto the priests.

And it was true that a certain man called Joseph had banded together ones that loved Jesus Christus, and sought out the Rome's halls and called audience with the mighty one. And Joseph had spoken words, pleading that the man,

Jesus Christus, be left unto the people. And he had told them the wrath of the Jews was high, for they knew that there was among them a man called Hatte, who was ill-begot of Tiberius, and no man raised his hands against him. Even had he spoken evil among the people and set them against the man Jesus. Even more spake he, that this man Hatte had oped the throat of Jacob, had oped sacks of grain and felled sheep. Yea, and had wrought havoc among the hill's-ways and even afar upon the ways unto Nazareth; even within the spot called Bethlehem had he done havocs, and yet, though he was taken unto Rome's pit, no thing had been done. And he spake that it should be done unto this one even before the flesh of Jesus had suffered else he would rouse the Jews.

And even as Joseph spake with the mighty one, lo, the sound of the coming of them that bore Jesus Christus sounded out, and they cried amid their laughter and shouting: "Crucify Him! Spread Him ope! Shew the men of Jerusalem their King, who hath called Him the Son of God!"

And they laughed and cast filth upon the tatters of Jesus Christus. And He walked among them, beaten as some waste upon a wave, seeing not, hearing not. And they came unto the walls of the Rome's halls, and they swept Him through the great gate unto the inner courts, thence unto the hall, even among the slaves and men of office, for they were hot of wines and wicked of heart. And the priests of the Jews fell fearful before such a sight, and they spake not nor cried out against Him.

And the men of office sought the side of the mighty one, and among them stood Arminius. And they that bore the form of Jesus Christus cast Him before them, and smote Him as they bore Him on. And they came them up unto the ope of the mighty hall and craved entrance. And it was true that they were left to come therein.

And they cried aloud: "Behold, sire, we have come forth from the judge of Galilee, and yet of the priests, with this man. He is a perverter of the people and is filling up the land with treasons against Rome."

And the mighty one looked upon Jesus Christus, whose flesh shewed the white bite of the lash and the blush beside it, and he was troubled. And he spake: "Thou hast brought Him forth and I have found Him not an offender, and even so, thou speakest, hath done the judge of Galilee. What then wouldst thou of me?"

And they cried out: "Hark, sire! Offer Him up beside the flesh of the man, Hatte. Give Him unto the hands of thy people, for the Jews are full of wrath against the man Hatte, and they hold him up. It is spoken that he is even the blood of Tiberius. This is a common thing. Rome is derided before Jerusalem. Make them lap up their words in blood! The priests have spoken words to undo Him and *they* are the law. The Jews dare not arise. Bring Him down!"

And it was true that the mighty one looked unto Jesus Christus and said: "What sayest thou?"

And He turned unto the priests and spake: "This day hast thou emptied the temple and stripped the tabernacle. Rome hath thee! Thou art as clay within her hands. Ye may not undo that that thou hast done. Oh weep, Jerusalem, for thou shalt cry unto the heavens to fall and cover thee! I say me, in the jealousy for thy God thou art consumed. In thy glut thou art stricken, for ye would feed the temple and make hungry the great God's hosts. Hereby thy blade of jealousy hath slain the lamb of sacrifice for the feeding of the tribes of ages. And Rome shall undo thee! Oh, ye priests of the temple, thou hast o'erturned thy urns of wisdom upon this people, and I say they have not drunk it! By thy hands of office is the altar made. Yea, and by thy blade the lamb is slain. Yea, but the brand of Rome lighteth the fire of sacrifice, and the stone of Rome hath keened the blade! Begone! for the voices of the priests of ages shall arise in an endless praying, and Rome shall stand holding up thy God for men to laugh upon, for He shall be dead within Rome's hands, by Rome's hands and thy blade! Go! Go!"

And He towered tall and pointed unto the way out the hall. And they followed His shewing.

And He turned slow unto the mighty one, saying: "No Jew is beneath thee, but Jesus Christus. Do the thing! He awaiteth."

And the hall was silent. And He stood, robed in tatters and the stripes of the thong, regal. And Rome cowered before Him.

And when He had stood long so, He turned, unto them that had taunted Him, a smile like unto a young sun of morning. And they feared Him. And the mighty one arose and spake naught, but bid that they bear Him thence, delivered unto the blade's men. And they bore Him from the great hall unto the pits' places.

And they that had come set their tongues living once more. And they spake like wild things: "Crucify Him! Crucify Him! Lay Him low! Bring forth the flesh of the man that oped the Jew's temples, and slay him! Yea, upon the feast day make ye merry, oh sire! Offer up sacrifice before the eyes of the Jews, lest they arise. Shew them Rome's heel!"

And the mighty one spake: "I will not of it."

And they made louder noises, even did they fall one unto the other. And the men of office of Rome spake unto him: "Seest thou? These men are of Rome, but they abide in Jerusalem and they shall raise up the Jews. It is a fearful tide. Deliver the man up."

And the mighty one arose and stood and bade that the slaves bring forth a cup, and he drank it slow and pondered. And he called that a slave bring forth a fount, and Indra went forth and returned with a bowl of gold and jade. And she offered it, and the mighty one arose and bathed him therein, saying: "This is a sign I will not of it."

And the men of office looked unto him, and he spake: "Do as thou wilt."

And they that had sought departed, filled up of the words of the men of office that they would deliver these up unto their hands upon the feast day.

And when the hour was late, behold, within the Rome's walls the pits' places were dark, and there had sounded out the step of them that brought one forth even unto the spot, and this was Jesus Christus. And they oped the pit and left Him therein. And He stood amid the dark, still, silent, still.

The Crucifixion of Jesus

22. And the first gray of day shewed.

And without, men sought amid the dark with lighted brands, and their voices sounded loud about the Rome's halls, and they spake fearfully. For some of them were Jews who watched, and some were of various tribes, and some were of Rome. And they of other tribes were Rome's. And they spake: "They shall be delivered up. This day shall they fall into the hands of them that seek them."

And amid the calling sounded out the words: "The Son of God!" "The King of the Jews!" "The Son of Tiberius!" "A swinenoble!" "Crucify them!" "Crucify them!"

And the ways ran of men who breathed fast, and dogs barked, and asses brayed, and the sounds of morning were wild.

And behold, the pits were oped, and they delivered unto the hands of the war's men, and they whom Rome had set mad, Jesus Christus and the son of Tiberius! And it was true that Rome had shut up her doors and left be that that would. And the sun was o'erclouded and shone but to hide. And the blade's men bore forth Jesus Christus, whom they had stripped naked, and He shrunk beneath their eyes and cast His eyes down. And lo, they laid hands upon Hatte and stripped him, and the women that looked upon this withdrew and hid.

And they cried out: "Who art thou, thou thief of the temples? Who art thou?"

And Hatte stood like unto one who wandered upon some far height. And they cried aloud: "Behold the son of Tiberius! Behold him!"

And they laughed and cast stones and bits of stone wares and rotted fruits and filths of the street's-ways. And Hatte stood, empty. And Jesus Christus spake not. And they decried Him, crying out: "Behold the King of the Jews! He is the son of who! He is a false prophet! Stone Him! Stone Him!"

And they lay hands upon them and beat them on the path's-way, even as wastes upon waters. And their flesh was torn and the hairs of their heads torn out, an lo, blood shewed upon their faces and their naked flesh. And the chill of the after-storm was upon Jerusalem, and they shook in cold quaking. And they that taunted them brought forth waters and cast o'er them; even did they bring forth heated brands and put unto their flesh.

And lo, among them stepped the Son of God, silent. They knew Him not. And Hatte held his head high and stepped regal, even though his withered leg gave way and was dragged at his stepping, for the weighting down of them that beset him was o'ermuch.

And they wearied of their taunts, for no manner of outcry came there for to feed their madness. And they cried out: "Crucify them! Spread them ope! Shew unto all men that enter the city, the Son of God and the son of Tiberius! Ha, ha, ha! Down the flesh of Rome beneath all men! Crush the blood of Tiberius beneath the heels of men where he hath crushed the flesh of our tribes!"

And it was true that the Jews were mad, and, mingled with the Romans within one cup; had they fallen. And when the cry had gone up "Crucify them!" behold, Hatte looked unto Jesus Christus, whose body was sagged of weakness, and with his own arms did he cast off them that clung, and tear him through flesh unto His side and lift Him up. And his lips spake: "Seest thou? It is the end of the paths. Thine of love and mine of hate lead thee unto a common thing."

And Jesus Christus lifted up His head, and behold, through the blood, through the sears of torment, through the agony of flesh, broke forth the smile of God. And Hatte looked upon His face, and his thin lips spread in smiling.

And they that looked upon this waxed wrath o'er their filling and beset one the other. Men fell upon their brothers, even did they deal flesh wounds one unto the other, so that blood was upon them as a hideous cloak.

And it grew dark, and lo, clouds rolled up like smokes of wrath, and the heavens flamed licking fires, and the thunders pealed upon them. And this but set the wraths frenzied more, and they went forth and brought unto the spot young trees and binded them up with thongs into rude crosses. And these were the work of wrath, and the woods were rough and the barks sharp. And lo, these they laid upon the backs of Jesus Christus and the son of Tiberius.

And Hatte took it upon him and murmured: "Is the God sleeping?" And he looked unto Jesus Christus, who sagged beneath the new weight, and he spake: "Thou, too, even as Tiberius, hath betrayed thy Son."

And behold, the flesh of Jesus gave way, and He sunk. And they lay scourges upon Him, and He might not arise, for the wine of the flesh was gone; His spirit chafed that it flee.

And Hatte called out loud: "Brother! Brother! I am calling!"

And Jesus arose, and lo, upon His face was the smile.

And the heavens roared like monstrous caves filled of wraths of ages. And the lightenings licked the earth, and the winds arose and blew like wild voices o'er the hill's-ways and valleys.

And they drove them upon the way unto a high spot, barren of shade, where the sun might bite. And it was true that there sounded out a wail of anguish, and it was the voice of Hatte, for he was broken. And from out the throngs sped a woman, crying: "Hatte! Hatte! Hatte!" And this was Mary,[1] who followed with the mother of Him. And lo, they wept, and were cast among the men as wastes, and beaten and trodden, yea, and bruised. And the cheek of Mary was white and stained; yea, even the things they had cast at the flesh of Jesus Christus and Hatte had smitten her and the holy bearer of Him. And lo, at the calling: "Hatte! Hatte!" Hatte arose and cried aloud: "Theia,[2] behold thy son! This is the long dark path, but the fleeing is no more! It is come! The hand of Tiberius hath fallen!"

And Mary came her up and with her frail hands made that she bear the cross, and wept and spake soft words, saying: "Wait! Wait! Rememberest thou? He shall come!"

And Hatte spake: "It must be true, for true as hate hath followed me hath this."

And lo, they swept them apart and trod down the women, leaving them, and bore them upon the way.

And when they had come unto the high spot, lo, already stood one cross made living![3] And they cast down Hatte and lay the cross upon the earth and brought forth irons. And they made him ready, and through the living flesh they set man's wrath to prison man's flesh unto God-wrought wood.

---

[1] Daughter of Flavius

[2] After losing his sanity, Hatte often mistook Mary, daughter of Flavius, for his mother Theia

[3] *The Sorry Tale* provides no background information regarding the crucifixion of this individual

And they took up the smitten hand and made ready. And Hatte laughed and spake: "It is dead!" And they brought forth the whole hand, and Hatte whispered hoarse: "It is whole! Behold, earth, I offer it unto thee!" And they made it fast and he cried: "Ye – oh! – will not!" And they fastened his feet. And his lips stopped, locked of agony, and his eyes spake empty.

And they cast down Jesus Christus. And behold, they had brought forth the tatters within which He had been clothed and they spread them forth and cried: "Behold, the raiment of a King!" And they took bits among them and cried aloud in mockery. And it was true that one who stood holding of the cloth saw it not. And this was Flavius.

And they lay upon Jesus Christus, and behold, Hatte's lips twisted that he speak, and the word was the watchword, "Mercy!" And he whispered: "God, if thou art God, mercy!"

And behold, the form of Jesus fell empty, knowing not, and they pierced the chalice that let flow the living wine. And they raised up the crosses and made them fast. And lo, the clouds sunk even upon the earth, sweeping the hills and breaking down the trees in wrath of the winds. And the tempest rang the wraths that should fall upon ages of them that did this thing.

And it was true that they stood beneath the crosses and beat upon the pierced feet, and the flesh quivered like unto a host of maggots beneath the skin. And behold, the ribs stood out even so that it seemed they would burst the flesh, and their bellies panted, and the eyes rolled from side unto side in anguish.

And when they had stood looking upon this long they lay hands upon the two women who sought. And it was true that women of the town had come that they lend their succor unto them that sorrowed. And they that had borne them up upon the crosses laid hands upon them and brought them up unto the foot of the crosses and cried: "Look upon the King of the Jews, women! Look upon Him! Look upon the flesh of Tiberius!"

And Mary sunk and tore unto shreds her mantle, crying out the while, and made that she bind up the wounded feet. And behold, their lips were stained of blood where they had kissed their loved flesh!

And the legs had split up unto the knees with the weighting down and the flesh-quaking which tore at the throbbing. And behold, there was a sound of anguish, and the body of Hatte fell forward, crushing, the hands torn loose and the knees broken. And they that looked sent up a shout of victory. Yea, their voices shrieked and mingled with the on-sweeping torrents. And they laid hold of him and made the cross low and binded him up once more.

And it was the late sun, and it glowed anger-red below the bellied clouds.

And lo, there sounded out a voice calling: "Oh-e-e-e!" For it had been true that the camel had come unto Jerusalem, and they had taken in word that they had borne the son of Tiberius forth for to crown. And Theia had been full of what her heart held and had followed their pointing, and behold, when she had come unto the spot her eyes took in the multitudes and the cries and the storm and fear was upon her. And lo, she came upon His loved, who stood afar, praying, after the manner He had spoken. And she had leaned far and said: "Where is the crowning of the son of Tiberius?"

And they answered: "Yon."

And she had looked upon what shewed on high o'er heads of the multitudes, and behold, her throat swelled, and she tore at her locks and her hands she beat one upon the other, speaking: "It *shall* be!" And lo, she sprang off the camel and ran swift. Like unto a bounding deer her feet sped in the beauteous steps of the dance. And she loosed her locks and brought forth the cloths and spread them, tearing off the mantle of coarse stuffs, and her lips speaking: "It shall be! It shall be!"

And lo, she came up unto the things that stood, dead things, empty chalices that dropped drops and that still made flesh sounds. And behold, the hands were swelled unto the blackening, and the lips were black of blood, and the heads sunk. And they that looked upon them called out: "Behold, the Son of God and the King of the Jews!"

And they brought forth a white script and with wet blood wrote: "The King of the Jews." And this hath n'er been wiped whither. And they cried out: "See the son of Tiberius! He is broken! He is no more! Crown him! Crown him! Yea, and the King, for their heads are still free and may suffer!"

And they brought thorned branches and wove crowns and with their hands pressed them down unto the deep of the flesh. And lo, they cried not out.

And the flesh of Hatte shook, and he made that he wet his lips with his tongue, and his throat made a hollow sound. And he turned his head unto Jesus Christus and called: "Brother, the sign!"

And no sound came. And the voice of Jesus, at a later time, cried out: "My God! My God! Hast thou forsaken me?"

And lo, Hatte bended his body like unto a bow and cried: "Behold the palms wave! The sands gleam! The caravan cometh, and it is led by a camel white as goat's milk, whose eyes are like unto rubies, and upon it – Jesus Christus! And before it danceth Theia! And one limpeth – Simeon! Simeon! Caanthus, I am strong!"

And he gave up the ghost.

And upon the cross still suffered He, for the transgressor of the Jews beside Him lived. And they that watched laughed, and behold, they saw that they stirred and they brought forth vinegar, the wine of the people, and offered it that He might live long to suffer.

And it was true that the Jews had fallen fearful, and one and another departed unto the temples to pray and hide. And Rome remained to glut upon the feast. And they had called out against the Son of God, and fallen weary of His words, for He forgave them, and spake in tones to the heavens, crying out that the Father forgive, for the Jews knew that Rome had lain their backs ope.

And the transgressor cried out long in his agony, and he turned unto Jesus Christus, speaking out: "Mercy!" And the Rome's men spake unto Him: "If thou art the Son of God, save thyself and him."

And the transgressor spake: "Why do this unto Him? He hath done naught unto thee, and I have perverted the laws and undone them."

And Jesus Christus turned His head slow unto the transgressor and spake: "Behold, thou shalt enter the new land this day and be with the Father even as I."

And lo, they looked upon Him at this, for He was uttering prophecy even in death.

And He hung, His beauteous head wet of blood and crowned of thorns, even as man had made His days thorned, and His precious flesh was illumined with the flames of the lightning.

And behold, the earth quaked. And it was true that the tombs gave up dead. Their bodies were shaken free. And when the mighty peal had fallen like a trumpet, like a bird that flees singing, sounded out: "It is finished!"

And His head sunk, and He turned unto the withered form of Hatte, hanging limp and broken, and the smile of God broke upon His countenance, and it was o'er.

Printed in April 2023
by Rotomail Italia S.p.A., Vignate (MI) - Italy